KITCHEN ESSAYS

Persephone Book Nº30
Published by Persephone Books Ltd 2001
Reprinted 2008 as a Persephone Classic

First published in 1922
by Thomas Nelson & Sons, reprinted from
The Times
© The Estate of Lady Jekyll

Endpapers taken from a printed silk, 'Clusters of stylised
fruits, flowers and shell motifs', designed by
George Sheringham for Seftons in 1922,
reproduced by courtesy of the Trustees of the
Victoria & Albert Museum, London

Typeset in ITC Baskerville by Keystroke,
Jacaranda Lodge, Wolverhampton

Printed and bound in Germany
by GGP Media GmbH, Poessneck

ISBN 978-1-906462-031

Persephone Books Ltd
59 Lamb's Conduit Street
London WC1N 3NB
020 7242 9292

www.persephonebooks.co.uk

KITCHEN ESSAYS:
WITH RECIPES AND THEIR OCCASIONS

by

AGNES JEKYLL

✳✳✳✳✳✳✳✳✳✳

PERSEPHONE BOOKS
LONDON

DEDICATED

TO MY DAUGHTERS

▼

" Here I have but gathered a nosegay of strange
floures, and have put nothing of mine unto it but
the thred to binde them."

Montaigne, Book III.

PREFACE

THESE short essays in cookery embody a number of recipes, treasure trove from many sources, collected during years of house-keeping under varied conditions. Their re-appearance in book form is due to requests from readers of *The Times* who have found them of practical use in kitchens where old-established standards and experience have in many cases disappeared during the recent years of upheaval.

Detailed directions for the fundamental processes of cookery are available in so many excellent books that a knowledge of ordinary kitchen practice has been here pre-supposed; but when homes dissolve and re-form, or the main prop of a household is withdrawn, it is often found that a good tradition or a valued formula, painstakingly acquired, has vanished beyond recovery, and that the pleasant things we enjoyed in youth, the unfamiliar foods which added interest to our travels abroad, or the *spécialité* of some clever long-lost cook, have all been swept irrevocably down Time's rolling stream.

This slight attempt at salvage is made for the benefit of those who come after, and if a few stray reflections have been thrown in with the salt and the sugar, it may be that, in the words of Lucretius, " One thing shall thus give light to another."

AGNES JEKYLL.

Midsummer to Easter, 1921–22.

CONTENTS

CONTENTS

KITCHEN ESSAYS

I

OLD FRIENDS WITH NEW FACES

"MY nature demands that my life should be perpetual Love," wrote dear Lord Beaconsfield to one of his female friends in a moment of spiritual expansion, and Dr. Swift recommended women to " turn their attention less to making nets, and more to making cages," so that there might be fewer unhappy homes.

Our mothers were apt to speak with almost brutal frankness about the way to the human heart ; and as its topography does not change, it may be well to give closer study to it, with a view to entering and entrenching ourselves firmly in that citadel. This can only be accomplished by persevering and intelligent effort. If, then, we would have laughter and shining faces at our board—if we would preserve the devotion of our husbands, the enthusiasm of our children, the preference of our friends, and the contentment of our domestics—let us as housekeepers give more of our best brains to the work. We must put those thoroughbreds, Imagination, Generosity, Invention, into harness with our jaded hacks, Custom, Thrift, and the Commonplace, as they drag along Time's hurrying chariot to the often depressing sound of the family gong.

It is the old friend greeting us in the piquant disguise of a new acquaintance that interests us, the unexpected that stimulates our listless appetite, begetting thereby brilliant talk and happy memories. For long industrious years have you not ordered weekly a Roast Leg of Mutton, inevitable as a mother-in-law, dreary as the weekly washing book ; but now . . . re-christen it *Gigot de Six Heures*, and having begged the butcher (who must be not your enemy

but your friend and ally) for a specially nice
small one—Welsh for choice, in compliment
to recent additions to our House of Lords—
ask your cook to treat it thus :—

> Stick into the thick part of the joint
> a refined little clove of garlic, cover the
> bottom of a braising pan, into which
> you have put a walnut-sized piece of
> fresh butter, with a liberal allowance of
> fresh vegetables, onions, carrots, celery,
> some thyme, parsley, and a bay leaf.
> Lay your gigot in the vegetables and
> fry quickly and thoroughly, turning the
> meat constantly so that it may brown
> well. Then add half a bottle of claret
> and a dash of brandy—if it can be
> spared—with a breakfast-cupful of good
> stock. Let these simmer gently from
> about 4 o'clock till dinner-time, basting
> the meat often. Before serving, strain
> the gravy from the vegetables, remove
> the clove of garlic, and place your gigot
> on a roomy dish, preferably of brown
> earthenware, and garnish this, pouring
> over the gravy, immediately after carv-
> ing it delicately, and handing it round,
> very hot, with some browned potatoes
> and any other vegetables liked, such
> as creamy turnips or braised haricots.

Soubise sauce is a good addition; and if the butcher is sympathetic and will let you have two calves' feet, well scalded and cleaned and cut up, to be added to the meat while braising, both your shares and the cook's will rise in the home market.

Your spinster aunt will certainly accuse you of undue extravagance after she has partaken freely of this dish. Score off her with a delicious and economical *Clear Consommé without Meat*, a household stand-by during the rationed, meatless years.

Fry in margarine or dripping a few carrots, turnips, 2 or 3 onions, and 2 bay leaves, add a teaspoon of " Marmite Vegetable Extract " (obtainable at Stores) to cold water in the quantity required—for four diners, say 4 large cups of water to a teaspoonful of marmite, or even less—and boil from 3 to 4 hours. Then strain and cut up the best of the flavouring vegetables as a garnish in the soup. Celery is an improvement, bay leaves a necessity.

After roast mutton comes our kind old friend rice pudding, but one which will be acclaimed at luncheon, even by the returned schoolboy, if invested with novelty and charm in the simple manner here and now set out, and re-baptized *Dundee*.

> Boil sufficient rice in milk until cooked rather firm, sweeten, and fill in therewith a fireproof glass or nice-looking pie-dish, adding a spendthrift's spreading of juicy home-made marmalade, and leaving a small valley in the centre for the following mixture to fill in : Butter, $2\frac{1}{2}$ oz., melted but not allowed to oil, adding to it, while warm, $2\frac{1}{2}$ oz. sugar and the yolks of 5 eggs mixed well together and beaten till light. Pour this all over. Bake in a not very hot oven from $\frac{1}{2}$ to $\frac{3}{4}$ hour. It should be a pleasant *café-au-lait* brown on the top, like the ideal sponge cake, and there should be enough for six people without the second helpings they will ask for, which are as inartistic as encores at the opera.

These two are familiar friends, but now comes an acquaintance from abroad in the shape of a summer luncheon sweet, popular in Sweden, under the name of *Röd-Grö*.

Boil currants and raspberries with a little water and sugar in the proportion of 2 lb. of fruit to a tea-cup of water and a ¼ lb. of white sugar. Pass through a sieve, and put it into an enamel stewpan with a large teaspoonful of sieved arrowroot, stirring gently but inexorably till smooth, when it should be of the consistency of gooseberry fool. Serve very cold, and if convenient, slightly iced, in shallow white china or cut-glass flat dish, and let plain fresh cream and either boiled rice or *petit choux* complete the offering.

After these two very simple but pleasing sweet dishes, here is another of a more recondite nature, *Russian Ice*, acquired from a Muscovite friend, and useful to those who can beg, borrow, or pluck from black-currant bushes a large handful of their youngest leaves.

These must be thrown into a pan of boiling syrup made in the proportion of ½ lb. white sugar to 1 pint water. Cover the pan and let it cool for 2 hours. Then strain, and add the juice of 6 lemons and freeze in the usual manner, as you would when making lemon water ice, which it will resemble in appearance, but the flavour a far more ethereal one and endued with the compelling power of the Blarney Stone.

This subtly flavoured sweet, served in pretty tall glasses, should have as followers a glass bowl of luscious black currant compote (freshly gathered, if possible; if not, the best bottled brand) and some crisp home-made Cat's Tongue Biscuits, or even the harmless useful sponge rusk out of a newly opened tin, to go round your table of six or eight fortunate guests on a hot summer evening.

From food to drink. Here is a pleasant " refresher," specially suitable for the young after lawn tennis or sports on hot days, but acceptable also to their elders when exhausted by church, depressed by gardening, or exasperated by shopping.

Raspberry Vinegar.

Take 1 lb. raspberries to every pint of best white vinegar. Let it stand for a fortnight in a covered jar in a cool larder. Then strain without pressure, and to every pint put ¾ lb. white sugar. Boil 10 minutes, let cool, and bottle in nice-shaped medium-sized bottles saved perhaps from some present of foreign liqueurs or scent. A teaspoonful stirred into a tumbler of water with a lump of ice, or introduced to a very cold syphon, will taste like the elixir of life on a hot day, and is as pretty as it is pleasant.

In some such ways as these—and there are many, many more—can affection won be kept alive and tender, and have we not the highest authority for knowing that without love we are nothing.

II

"LE MOT JUSTE" IN FOOD

" NEVER the time and place and the loved one
all together " sang our poet of the intellect,
which, translated into terms of the menu,
should indicate a desirable combination of the
appropriate dish at the right moment with
the particular individual. Therein lies the
golden opportunity for the wits of the housekeeper, who should study the meteorological
forecasts with the anxiety of a yachtsman or
a mountaineer, and try to recall both the pet
aversions and the preferences of those for
whom she is catering. There was once a
man who actually swore when lobster and
crab were offered to him on successive days
at luncheon, and refused all food on the
third day at sight of mushrooms, for these
all disagreed with him poisonously. He was

19

a J.P. and a churchwarden too! One guest scored off a solicitous hostess who, when accepting a proffered visit for luncheon, asked for some guidance as to the then preferred diet—was it vegetarian or uncooked fruit, were vitamines and proteids desired or taboo? The reply came short and incisive: "Thank you, I eat everything except *corpses*," thereby making a lamb cutlet or the wing of a boiled chicken seem positively tigerish. Some people let their moderation be known to all men, never, according to their own account, partaking of anything grosser than twelve almonds and six raisins in the twenty-four hours. Others boast of a cup of milk with two slices of brown bread and a lettuce. Do not fear overmuch to put such resolution to the test. They have been known often to enjoy copious and diversified meals—only their doing so must never be noticed.

Here is an excellent luncheon dish under the name of *Dutch Omelet*, accepted by various sects and creeds with apparent relish both on feast and fast days, to be made thus :—

> Prepare some batter with milk, flour, and 4 yolks of eggs. Whisk the whites well, but do not let it get too stiff in mixing. Make a fairly thick pancake, with a soufflé strain in it and not too much done, and spread it in the large round deep plated dish in which it is to be served. Keep it at the mouth of the oven, and sprinkle it liberally with grated parmesan. Make a second pancake and lay it on the top, sprinkling delicately with finely - chopped ham. Add yet a third pancake on the top of these, and put over and around asparagus tops or green peas. The large white asparagus of good brand, bottled, or the cheaper tinned variety, will serve in the desolate months when the real thing is unprocurable. Cover the whole with a good creamy white sauce and serve very hot.

Turn your thoughts to a tropical week-end in July or August, when you might expect a jaded Cabinet Minister or a depressed financier, a critic from the Foreign Office or an epicure from the Guards Club, and

KITCHEN ESSAYS

try them with this *Selle d'Agneau à la Mira-mar*. It is not exactly a cheap dish, but we are told to cast our bread upon the waters and that we shall find it after many days : it might conceivably induce a rich legacy from a bachelor uncle.

Take a nice juicy saddle of lamb, or mutton, trim it from skin and super-fluous fat. Roast it carefully and let it get cold. Then cut out the fillets on either side of the backbone and mask these thinly with aspic jelly on the top. The space left is to be covered in with a cold *mousse*, for which use a piece of freshly cooked lamb about 1 lb. in weight, cleaned of fat and sinew, cut very small and then pounded in a mortar with ¼ lb. fresh butter, passed through a sieve and mixed with a little cream *half whisked*. Add a little Purée of Foie Gras (tins about 1s. 8d. at Stores). Put this mix-ture into the excavations on either side of the saddle, let it set, and cover with thin aspic jelly. If the purée should be too stiff, moisten with jelly, cream, or a little velouté sauce. Cut as many slices, long and thin, from the fillets as are required ; lay them across the saddle

22

resting on the backbone. Serve on a roomy dish surrounded with lettuce leaves in which are put a garnish of fruit salad. Serve very cold.

For this same festive and hot week-end, capture a stately pineapple. But do not waste it at dessert, when most guests will gladly exchange the heat and effort of the dining-room for the scented *solitude à deux* of the star-lit garden. Use it for a combined entremet and fruit course, cutting it in half through the crown of leaves downwards, then scoop out the fruit, and make it into a very good water or cream ice in the usual way. One hollowed-out side of pineapple, lying lengthwise on a silver dish, will be filled with this, the other with a fairly stiff compote of red cherries, fresh or bottled. Those put up with maraschino or in heavy syrup are popular. Serve with this, freshly baked *Cat's Tongue Biscuits.* Here is the jealously guarded formula :—

Two oz. white sugar, 2 oz. fine pastry flour, mixed together with fresh cream, and a little milk well flavoured with vanilla pod added. Force this mixture through a forcing bag on to a greased baking sheet in long 8-inch lengths, narrow as a little finger, but splaying out into a heavy thumb at either end. After 5 to 10 minutes in a hot oven they should be of a deep cream colour, merging along their edges into the delicate brown of fading magnolias.

If the week-end guests should arrive in time for tea, offer them this *Cut Gooseberry Preserve*, the triumph of a Scottish jam-maker of wide renown in the Borders. They need not be put off by recollections of the sour pip-infected mash which often disgraces the homely label.

Take 7 lb. unripe gooseberries—" Sulphur " is the best variety for the purpose. They must not be hard, nor yet too ripe. Top and tail them and cut in halves straight across. Scoop out seeds with wrong end of a teaspoon. Cover with 1½ pint cold water, and boil for ½ hour. Strain through a hair sieve or cheese-cloth. Weigh the

24

cut gooseberries, and allow to each pound of fruit 1 lb. best loaf sugar. Weigh the juice also, and allow weight for weight of sugar. It then takes from $\frac{3}{4}$ to 1 hour to boil to a nice rich red colour in which the now soft gooseberry skins are merged in close but separate units.

Do not forget the now ripening *Morello Cherries*, which, drowned in brandy, made such irresistible appeal as winter dessert in pre-war days. If brandy be still ruled out by the well-balanced mind, try bottling them in good Marsala and sugar in sterilized bottles with wide mouths and screw-on tops. Bring them thrice over just to the boil, withdrawing quickly, and finally corking to the exclusion of all air. Pussyfoots love them served in glasses with becoming caps of fluffy cream, and will mellow visibly under their influences, sweet as those of the Pleiades.

III

IN THE COOK'S ABSENCE

" NEVER hesitate to do a kind action," said a cynical friend once in the writer's privileged hearing. " The burden of it almost invariably falls on some one else, whilst you get all the credit." The truth of this dictum, once heard, will often recur to the mind when promising, shall we say soup, or jelly, to some sick friend ; for it is the cook who will make the offering, the boy who will carry it to its destination. Gifts of flowers and greenery generously pressed on a London bound guest, choice cuttings or herbaceous plants promised to the gardening enthusiast—do we ourselves rise early to gather them ? do we personally divide and label, pack and despatch, that hamper, or is it the already hard-worked gardener ? The generous offer of a new dress-pattern, the formula for a knitted jumper, the recipe for an attractive cake or dish—do we always measure and copy out ourselves, or set some one else to work, whilst we warm our cold hearts with unearned gratitude ? Recent wedding festivities in a cherished neighbour's home were the cause of an offer made with a light heart, and deeply regretted when it caused the temporary absence of her from whom depended much of the peace and comfort of the home. This time culprit and kitchen-maid were joint sufferers. A capable damsel with a record of highly paid service in a Labour Bureau, but inexperienced in matters of the kitchen, promised to rise to the occasion after a course of suggestive psycho-analytical treatment. As similar experience may befall many of us, particularly at busy holiday times of the year, when cooks, whose mothers so often specialize in sudden and disastrous illnesses, may leave us to face problems we have never really envisaged before, it may be well to anticipate such emergency.

KITCHEN ESSAYS

A vision of the pleasant spacious kitchen of a small French inn visited in a recent motor tour came to the rescue. The shining utensils, the gay earthenware, the charming patronne, all recalled the savour of an excellent brew whose evolution she obligingly encouraged her guest to study. This, if it could be recaptured, should welcome coming guests and cause the artist's temporary absence to be forgiven. It was called *Garbure à la Lionnaise,* and may be accomplished thus :—

Chop some onions finely, and place, with 2 oz. of fresh butter, on a moderate fire in a frying pan till browned. Cut 8 or 10 small slices from a long milk roll of bread, lay them in a fireproof glass or shallow earthenware dish, powdering in a little cheese first. On each slice of bread put a little of the cooked onion and a dusting of cheese—preferably half parmesan and half gruyère. Pour over these a glass of consommé or good stock (thoughtfully left ready by the absent artist), put the dish in the oven to brown, and if necessary pass a salamander over it just before serving it together with a marmite pot of hot consommé or good stock in the proportion of 1 quart for six people, adding 2 yolks of eggs and ½ glass of cream. Serve the garbure and the soupe simultaneously but in separate dishes.

For a fish course for six try this version of *Lobster à la Newburg*, which has many variants, this simple but acceptable one being best when daintily served in white china ramekin cases of fair size, and attended by thin gossamer slices of bread dried to lacy crispness in a slow oven :—

Take 1½ large cupfuls of cooked lobster, cut into pieces 1 inch square, 1 tablespoonful of butter, ¾ cup of Madeira or light sherry, 1 cup of fresh cream, the yolks of 2 eggs, some salt, a dash of pepper, and, if possible, 1 chopped truffle (or peelings as sold at Stores in small inexpensive glasses will do). Put the butter in a spotless stewpan with the lobster and truffle, salt and pepper, cover, and let simmer for 5 minutes. Add the wine, and cook for 3 minutes more. Have ready the yolks and cream well beaten, and add to the lobster,

29

shaking the pan until the mixture thickens, then serve at once.

This is so sure of success that the new kitchen-maid will feel encouraged to try her hand at *Biftecki à la Russe* :—

Some juicy and tender beefsteak in the proportion of 1½ lb. to six people, finely minced in a machine with the pipe affixed. Fry a little onion till nicely browned, adding a little stock (or bovril), and reduce somewhat. Add the minced meat, all gristle and skin carefully trimmed away, with salt and pepper to taste, and stir in ¼ pint of cream (Ideal milk is a possible substitute). Form into rounds, large as the tops of coffee cups and about 1 inch thick, flour lightly and fry in butter for some 10 minutes, pour over a little good gravy, and dish with grated horse-radish liberally dropped on each round, garnishing the flat dish which holds them with hot beetroot chopped into inch cubes, or with daintily cooked peas or beans.

The *Morello cherries* so beautifully embalmed in *Marsala and sugar* (see page 25) might complete this effort ; and as the

IN THE COOK'S ABSENCE

kitchen - maid will by now have warmed to her work, let her try her hand at these delicious *Orange Jumbles* to go round with the glasses of fruit and cream :—

> Take $\frac{1}{4}$ lb. shredded almonds, $\frac{1}{4}$ lb. white sugar, 3 oz. butter, 2 oz. flour, grated rind and juice of 2 oranges, and a soupçon of cochineal to colour all. Mix and put on a slightly greased baking tin in quantities of about 1 teaspoon to each jumble, allowing room to spread, and bake in a moderate oven. They will be the size of teacup rims, and should curl their crisp edges, faintly pink as the underneath of a young mushroom.

Leaving these instructions before your kitchen-maid's eyes, the sound of your stimulating words of hope and faith in her ears, you will be able, as hitherto, to transfer most of the burden on to her shoulders, and go up to dress for dinner, feeling that you have done your duty ; but, as Mrs. Wharton told us in a recent admirable novel, "the worst of doing one's duty is that it unfits us often for doing anything else."

31

IV

OF GOOD TASTE IN FOOD

No double meaning lurks in this heading, but it is not recognized perhaps as generally as it might be that the selection, preparation, and service of food have their own codes of fitness and quality, their rules governing cause and result, which cannot be ignored or transgressed without detriment to all concerned. Too much effort given to material things entails neglect of spiritual ones, too little induces loss of temper, money, and health. Some rare spirits there are who may discipline themselves into indifference to creature comforts, who may write magical poetry on lumpy porridge, paint glorious pictures on indifferent eggs, lead armies to victory on bully beef—we salute them and pass on ! But with those who,

32

whilst lifting reverential eyes to the stars, yet know and love this kind, warm earth, we would take counsel awhile. It is not thought praiseworthy to wear nasty clothes, to have ugly flowers in the garden, dull books on the table, comfortless furniture in the home, and horrid pictures on the walls. Why, then, are God's good gifts of food and drink to be spoiled by stupidity and mismanagement ? The French are artists in these matters, and yet of France it is said—

"A country that can think, and, thinking, acts ;
A country that can act, and, acting, dreams—"

Let us not, then, be too highbrow to learn something both theoretically and practically about food and cookery, or too lazy to take trouble anew every morning ; neither let us be so timorous as to sit down under a rule of what a schoolboy friend in a recent examination paper alluded to as " that practice introduced by the Greeks of a man having only one wife which is called *Monotony*."

KITCHEN ESSAYS

The dishes which will befit a king's banquet or a Lord Mayor's feast look strange and out of place in modest surroundings. Turtle soup, plum-pudding, and champagne for an August Sunday luncheon in a seaside villa would be, to say the least, incongruous, but have been experienced.

A blue-blooded and conservative marquis may be forgiven his temporary loss of self-control when the newly-engaged cook sent on its gay career round a decorous dinner-party of county neighbours a transparent and highly decorated pink ice pudding concealing within inmost recesses a fairy light and a musical box playing the " Battle of Prague." Words were spoken, and, like the chord of self in Locksley Hall, this over-elaborated creation " passed in music out of sight."

Matters of taste must be felt, not dogmatized about. A large cray-fish or lobster rearing itself menacingly on its tail seems quite at home on the sideboard of a Brighton hotel-de-luxe, but will intimidate a shy guest at a small dinner-party. A story quoted by Sydney Smith from an old chronicle records a dinner prepared for a meeting of bishops at Dort, one of the dishes being " a roasted peacock, having in lieu of tail the arms and banners of the Archbishop, which was a goodly sight to such as favour the Church." What a contrast to the practices prevailing in even the more stately homes of the Anglican clergy ! A great prelate of our own day is said to be contemplating drastic changes in a home life rendered difficult by the limitations of his cook, whose only alternative to a burnt offering, as he complained, was a bleeding sacrifice.

Over-elaboration then, even in our kindest cooks, must be discouraged : games of dominoes played in truffles over the chicken cream, birds' nests counterfeited round the poached eggs, jazzing jellies, and castellated cakes show misdirection of energy. Not that an occasional exception may not prove the rule—let it be made on behalf of *Gelée Crème de Menthe*, an emerald-green pool,

35

set in a flat glass bowl, reminiscent of Sabrina fair in her home below translucent waves, or of Capri caverns, cool and deep ; whilst the delicate aroma of peppermint will recall to Presbyterian minds those Sabbath indulgences practised by young and old at kirk in far-off Highland glens.

> Make a quart of good lemon jelly in the approved way, preferably with calves' feet, more probably with best leaf gelatine, but not—oh ! not—with jelly powders. Whilst warm add a handful of those large green peppermint geranium leaves, thick as a fairy's blanket, soft as a vicuna robe, and to be found in most old-fashioned gardens, and let them flavour your blend ; or you can use 3 or 4 drops of essence of peppermint, $\frac{1}{2}$ teaspoonful of apple green to colour, or home-made spinach greening for a substitute. Pass through your jelly bag and serve very cold. A glass of crème de menthe might well improve this, but is by no means indispensable.

To mollify the fastidious purist or placate the peppermint hater, prelude this recipe with an excellent *Consommé Fausse Tortue*. Elderly aldermen will bless you for it, and the hunters home from the hill will forget the rigours of the chase, and be warmed and comforted.

> Having removed the brains from half a calf's head, put it in a stewpan with a little salt and water to cover, and bring it to the boil, then place it under cold water tap and thoroughly wash. Put it back into the clean stewpan with enough stock or stock water to cover it, plenty of stock vegetables, also bay leaf, and a few allspice. Simmer gently for 5 hours, then strain, and leave to set. Next day remove fat, and clarify, adding a turtle tablet and some turtle soup herbs as sold at Stores. When clear, strain through a clean cloth, re-boil, add a little sherry, salt, pepper, to taste, and, just before serving, some pieces of the meat cut in gelatinous squares from the head and indistinguishable from green fat, two for each portion, of which there might be eight.

This would be a propitious moment for asking some favour, dropping out casually a regrettable piece of news, or even confessing to the near advent of an unwelcome visitor. It is wonderful how safely awkward corners can be turned and dangerous seas navigated without disaster if only the tactful moment be chosen for the venture.

V

ON THE SERVING OF FOOD

CICERO said that the worst peace is better than the justest war. We, who still suffer from both, may be thankful that at least the intricate mechanism of our daily lives has been a good deal simplified as their result. We have grown accustomed to shorter meals, and to prefer them,—to do without things which we now realize were never necessities. Servants being fewer, we have schooled ourselves to a greater measure of self-help, and the stately major-domo, once specially recommended as being able to " calve well off the table," would find that in many homes his occupation was gone. It is all the more incumbent to write with invisible ink on our menu cards " Little and good," and to see that the dishes, though few, are perfectly prepared and attractively presented.

Those who have persuaded their cooks to send things up as far as possible in the fireproof dishes or oven-glass in which they can often be admirably cooked, or appetisingly finished off, as well as served, will not willingly revert to that destructive transfer from cosy casseroles to chilly silver or china dishes, thereby depriving themselves of that good savour of the fire which lurks in brown marmites, but never penetrates into the glacial tureen. A few pounds spent in the sort of ware used in French and Italian restaurants, an occasional plunge for some of the beautiful china and glass specialities of our own admirable factories, which may be made to serve as Christmas or birthday presents in the family, the rash purchase of some alluring piece of pottery abroad, devastating, perhaps, as a travelling companion, but for ever after precious as a souvenir—these are amongst the extravagances we never regret.

ON THE SERVING OF FOOD

It is a poor encouragement to the cook to let her carefully-prepared, well-garnished dish cool its heels, first on a dinner lift, then behind a screen, where it is dealt with by an intermediary hand, and at last presented, often in fragments of unrecognizable derivation and uninviting appearance, its tardy companions, the gravy and sauce boats, the savoury rice or dressed vegetables, for which it called out long but in vain, never coming, like wisdom, until too late. Delay is almost invariably fatal to success, but a pair of carvers near the kitchen fire and a lightning flight straight to the dinner-table lend an unimagined savour to the simplest food. The sudden irruption of an anxious chef through a dining-room door bearing a soufflé light as thistledown, and crying apprehensively as he came, " Vite ! vite ! messieurs, mesdames, cela tombe ! cela tombe ! " was more than justified by the fleeting perfection of his *chef-d'œuvre*.

For luncheon try these *Rognons à la Turbigo* in a brown shallow fireproof dish, round

for choice, in which they can be finished
and served :—

> Clean some mutton kidneys of their
> outer skins, cut out hard centres and
> slice in large thin pieces, season and
> fry quickly in butter, and transfer to
> the dish in which they will be handed
> round—adding some already cooked
> mushrooms and some midget sausages,
> or slices of cipolata sausages already
> grilled. Pour over these a well-seasoned
> tomato sauce and some half-glaze mixed.
> Re-heat all together and serve piping
> hot.

For those who shudder at the idea of
kidneys, here is an unusually popular form of
Savoury Rice, which will taste all the better
if it comes straight from the oven in a brown
earthenware vessel, such as would be met
with in a humble French restaurant or on a
Dutch market-place :—

> One cupful Carolina rice, 4 tomatoes,
> 1 onion chopped fine, 2 potatoes, 2
> chicken livers cut up, 2 tablespoonfuls
> chopped ham. Put rice in a stewpan,
> cover with cold water, close tightly,
> stand on side of stove, and let it swell

thoroughly. Fry in clarified butter the onion, livers, and ham. Cut the two large potatoes and tomatoes into dice ; do not fry them. Put the fried onion, livers, ham, potatoes, and tomatoes into the brown casserole, about half fill with good brown stock, and let it simmer gently for 10 minutes, by which time the rice should be done and can be added to the casserole, and all well stirred together. Finish cooking in the oven with the lid on for 20 minutes. When done there should be a skin slightly brown over the top, but below it should be moist and succulent.

A round flat " oven-glass " dish will fitly hold *Cambridge Crème Brûlée*, long the exclusive speciality of a certain college, and served on any festal occasion with or without a bowl of fruit compote in its wake.

Boil 1 pint of good rich cream for a minute, pour it on to yolks of 4 eggs well beaten, replace on fire, and let it boil again. Then pour it into the dish in which it is to be served, which, if not of fireproof glass, might be one of those brown yellow French dishes imitating a pastry *croûte*. Let it get cold. Strew a thick coating of castor sugar over it, brown with a salamander, and serve very cold. A thin semi-transparent crackling top-crust should thus be formed over the yellowish custardy cream below, to be easily broken by a few sharp spoon taps before helping. A cold rice pudding for home luncheon in summer may be treated with sugar, and salamandered in the same way.

Brown earthenware soup pots with covers and saucers are excellent for serving up all homely soups, recipes for which are already simmering for a future chapter.

By ways such as are here suggested we may hope to escape the classical censure directed against that dinner tersely described as " ill chosen, ill cooked, ill carved, and ill served."

VI

CHILDREN'S BREAD

" WHEN I was little," said one of riper years,
" the peaches were all kept for the grown-up.
Now I am a grown-up, they are all given to
the children." It is the old, old story : jam
every other day—yesterday—to-morrow—
never to-day—which is what, on reflection,
makes it jam. Though the prevalent pre-
cedence of the young opens what Treasury
Minutes are fond of calling " a very serious
door," the elders can but enter and take
their back seats, waiting for that inevitable
swing of the pendulum which demonstrates
the fixity of Nature's laws.

Summer holidays are a suitable moment
for taking thought for our young, and for
adding, by good diet, at least one cubit to
their statures, for often even the best school

dietary fails to provide sufficient creamy milk, fresh butter, and other palatable fat-making foods so good for most young, and oftener still, opportunities for sufficient sleep and rest militate against their successful absorption. Let us think, then, how we can tempt the delicate appetite of the weaklings without stimulating the grosser ones of the greedy ; how combine nourishing simplicity with inviting wholesomeness. A grand-father recalls being admonished in his youth against ever showing surprise, or making any comment, even were a roasted elephant to be placed upon the table—a council of perfection, surely, for an unlikely contingency, though the writer remembers hearing a little boy of seven, born and brought up in the Faroe Islands, asking the waiter politely at his first dinner in an Edinburgh hotel if the proffered viand was beef or *whale* !

The children of to-day are seldom disciplined with the severity of the older generation, or bewildered by that tormenting though truthful alternative of our childhood—" those that ask, don't get ; those that don't ask, don't want " ; the good things of the table, like those of the eye and of the mind, being offered to them in easy profusion as compared to the stricter limitations of an earlier age. Who shall say that the reign of liberty and fraternity has not as good results ultimately as the reign of law ? The children of Israel reached the Promised Land after forty austere years in the wilder-ness, with little to eat and less to drink, displeasure prevailing above, murmurings below, yet we read that later they attained to greatness and prosperity on a diet of mammoth grapes and abundant wine, of overflowing milk and honey. The starved appetite waxes rapacious and greedy, the pampered youth grows soft and spoilt. These are highly controversial matters, and being generally questions of degree, can hardly reach very definite solution. Perhaps sympathy is what the young need most and thrive on best, and Mrs. Norton's answer to the child whom she had been set to

amuse, and had made friends with so successfully that it asked her : " Please, are
you very, very young too ? " will encourage
the elderly. " Yes, very, *very* young," she
answered. " But then, my dear, I have been
very young for a very long time."

Children's tastes, like their religion, are
oftenest simple and instinctive. " Chicking,
please," is still the birthday choice in most
homes, and let us not fail them in the matter
of *Bread Sauce*, of which there never is and
can hardly be enough. This is so much
oftener badly made and nasty, instead of well-
made and nice, that a few precepts for the
inexperienced hand, to which it is oftenest
entrusted, may not be amiss here. The
bread must be stale and grated from a tin
loaf, the milk good, and flavoured by boiling
in it till soft a large onion cut into fair-sized
pieces, and removed just before the milk is
poured on to the dry crumbs. This is the
moment to add a few removable peppercorns to simmer in a china cooking vessel
for some twenty minutes, adding more milk

as the bread absorbs it. A walnut of fresh butter stirred in before serving, and when peppercorns are removed, must not be omitted. Two teacups of crumbs to half a pint of milk, rising to three-quarters of a pint, should be a suitable allowance for four or five people.

Rosy-cheeked apples are what tempted Tommy on that fine summer day, even as his first progenitor, to sin. Next time you order that fruit of temptation for the young (and remember also that they are the favourite food of gouty millionaires), let them be peeled and stewed into *Spiced Purée of Apples*, with a liberal allowance of finely shredded citron or mixed peel, some allspice, and a dozen or more removable cloves. Or if you prefer *Apples Baked*, serve them on rounds of neglected sponge cake, fried crisp and spread generously with quince preserve. Or for *American Apples*, pour into their cored-out centres an overflowing baptism of maple syrup, which should also go round hot in a sauce-bowl instead of brown sugar, but not instead of cream. Or again, for *Apples Brésil* boil three tablespoonfuls of large bullet tapioca for from three to four hours in a pint of lemon-peel flavoured milk. Stew six cored, peeled, and sweetened apples, cut in segments. When both are cooked, put some of the tapioca in a deep glass fireproof dish, cover with half the apple, add the rest of the tapioca and fruit, and anoint liberally with apricot jam, and cook for twenty minutes in the oven. Your guests will never say they dislike those viscous spheres again.

A Tyrolese hostess once introduced an appreciative young party to what was regrettably called *Kaiserschmarren*, our old friend the pancake in its solider form, chopped into small pieces and put on a long flat dish into which she had shaken a couple of handfuls of sultanas warmed and soaked for some hours in a little white wine, dusted with sugar and cinnamon, and a sauce-boat of hot white wine syrup accompanying it. Pussyfoots could substitute a lemon juice syrup.

CHILDREN'S BREAD

Etonians will remember the chilly welcome given to those ungraceful rolls of suet pudding accompanied by inadequate treacle, and known to their hungry youth as " Aunt's Leg," or, in its saucepan-shaped variety, as " Haynes' Hat," reminiscent of those furry concertinas worn as head coverings by their younger contemporaries. The same materials can be treated according to the formula of a well-loved Scotch aunt, and how different the result ! Try this recipe for *Baked Roly-Poly* :—

Two breakfast cups of flour, $\frac{1}{2}$ lb. of suet shredded, 1 teaspoonful of baking powder, 2 teaspoonfuls of Demerara sugar. Mix into a very stiff paste with a little milk ; roll out not too thin, spread thickly with jam (stoneless damson or plum for choice), roll up, and brush with beaten egg. Butter a baking tin at one side only, tilt the tin inside the oven, bake in moderate heat from $\frac{1}{2}$ to $\frac{3}{4}$ hour. Should it spread whilst cooking, push into shape with a palette knife. Serve with additional warmed jam.

Another easily made and excellent sweet suitable for a young people's luncheon party can be warmly recommended under the name of *Berbage Pudding* :—

> Take ¼ lb. of bread crumbs, chopped suet, moist sugar, a pinch of salt, ½ teaspoonful of carbonate of soda, 3 heaped tablespoonfuls of strawberry jam, and 1 egg, all mixed well together and steamed in a brick-shaped mould for 4 hours. Turn out, and serve with the addition of a light mousseline sweet sauce poured over it or a good strawberry jam syrup around.

Well-brought-up children are trained to say grace, which recalls the memory of a Scotch minister, accustomed to share the mid-day meal of some of his flock between services. He varied his grace according to the feelings evoked by the fare set before him. Before fresh herrings, a dish he cordially disliked, he would begin, " For the least of all these Thy mercies," whereas roasted goose or duck with apple sauce moved him to a more fervid thanksgiving, beginning

CHILDREN'S BREAD

" Bountiful Creator." The simple grace said daily throughout the King's Navy, " Thank God "—accompanied by a hearty thump on the table—may well follow these last children's dishes, and grown-ups have been known to join with them in grateful appreciation.

VII

FOR MEN ONLY

OLD prejudices die hard, and even before the days of Martha, cumbered with her much serving, the kitchen was looked on as specially the woman's sphere of influence. Yet those who have been privileged to stay in bachelor households or to dine at restaurants with their men friends, will often admit their superlative capability both in running the domestic machinery with noiseless and well-oiled efficiency and in ordering a better dinner from a chef or maitre d'hôtel than most women would be able to achieve.

What female intelligence can decipher rapidly those hieroglyphic sheets when presented in restaurants and unerringly select the "spécialité de la maison," or the most acceptable "plat du Jour"? She will vacillate between the super-strange and the ultra-commonplace, or, losing her head, will select the cheapest of the mysteries proffered, or else plunge recklessly for something expensive and out of season. Sydney Smith boasted of his custom of stopping his female servant when encountered in the passage and asking her suddenly " whether she preferred duck or chicken ? " in order that she might acquire the good habit of swiftly making up her mind. Perhaps the old nursery game of Oranges and Lemons may conceal some such educative value, but choosing well is one of the most difficult things in a difficult world, seeing how profoundly it may affect our whole moral and physical well-being, whether applied to food, drink, companionships, or occupations, and that always our " Choice is brief and yet endless." Some people will never learn to choose, but, like the child at the birthday party asked what it would like to have, say, " A little of everything, please." That way madness lies.

55

Nor, gentlemen, is your efficiency confined to the ordering of meals ; it is shown also in your rapid diagnosis of a difficult situation, in your successful handling of individual psychology. A domestic crisis involving the immediate disappearance of the entire kitchen staff from a remote country house, filled to overflowing with three cheerful generations of holiday makers was narrowly averted one August by prompt and successful male action. Shortage of water, absence of coal, conflicting milk claims between rival nurseries, momentary loss of temper on the part of the principals, and disaster seemed imminent and irretrievable. " But what did you say to them all ? " asked a trembling and defeated mistress when he returned cheerfully from the back regions. " If you are a sensible woman, and I think you are, you will never ask or try to find out," was the enigmatical reply. But, anyhow, the barometer was set fair, and the dinner that night specially successful. Was it flattery ? Was it largesse ? Was it that combination

56

of a square jaw and a twinkling eye which
is often so persuasive ? No one will ever
know, but the kitchen was a place of sunshine
after storm, and the cook even volunteered
to write out for one appreciative guest these
recipes for her best efforts ; so whatever
the guilty secret, it was surely a case of
justification by works, and only a man could
have so handled the situation. Do not let
September pass without trying each one of
these dishes, all well suited to the season.

Clear Tomato Soup.

Cut in slices 1 lb. fresh tomatoes, and
put into enough ordinary clear soup for,
say, six people ; simmer gently for 1
hour, strain through a clean cloth, re-
boil, and serve with fried croutons,
about two-shilling-piece size, piled with
stiffly whipped cream, one to each person
on a separate plate. The cream softens
the acidity of the tomatoes and greatly
improves the flavour.

Perdrix aux Choux.

Take 2 partridges and prepare in usual
way. Old birds can be utilized in this

57

recipe if necessary. Braise them carefully with plenty of vegetables and stock for 1½ hour. Take a red cabbage, shred it finely, and put in boiling water for 5 minutes. Strain, and put in a casserole with a breakfast cup of good stock, a dessertspoonful of French vinegar, an onion, some fat bacon cut in small pieces, a dessertspoonful of castor sugar. Stir well, and stew or braise for an hour. Take out the onion, and heap at either end of a long hot dish with the birds in the centre. For more than four people increase the quantities.

Syston Iced Pudding.

Cut a sponge cake, the size of the mould to be used for pudding, in slices— a brick shape about 8 inches by 4 inches is good. Soak the cake with brandy and sherry. Prepare some stiffly whipped cream, sweetened and flavoured with brandy, and lay it in the mould alternately with dried glacé and brandied cherries between each layer of cake. Fill the mould full, cover in with buttered paper, and freeze 3 hours. Make a purée of apricots, with jam or bottled fruit, add brandy or sherry, or a little

58

curaçoa flavouring, put in the ice box
to become very cold, and pour round
the pudding.

Camembert in Aspic.

To 1 pint brown stock add a little
carrot, onion, celery, parsley, and a few
pimentoes (allspice), 1 dessertspoonful
of tarragon vinegar, 1 teaspoonful of
Worcester sauce, about 8 leaves of
gelatine, and 2 whites of eggs. Whisk
all together in a stewpan, place on
stove, bring slowly to the boil. When
clear strain through a fine cloth into
a basin. Remove the paper covering
from a ripe camembert and slightly
scrape it. Select a round tin a little
larger than the cheese and pour in the
liquid aspic to 1 inch in depth ; let it
set. Then place the cheese in the tin,
pouring in sufficient liquid aspic to
cover it ; leave it to set. Turn out
when ready, garnish with watercress
sprigs, and serve with thin oven-dried
crisp toast. Cream cheese can be
treated thus, and ice is not a necessity,
only in hot weather it takes longer to
set the aspic without it.

VIII

THOUGHTS OF VENICE FROM HOME

WE are admonished by philosophers to
remove our thoughts from any bliss that is
unattainable, but their balanced minds are
oblivious perhaps of the happiness to be
obtained, and without price, from retro-
spective enjoyment, or of the powers recently
discovered by Monsieur Baudoin to be
lurking within the practice of auto-sugges-
tion. To such as have longed each summer,
in vain, to take their holiday in Venice—to
such as have returned thence, but are still
under the spell of her magic—are these lines
addressed.

Certain great moments of life can live
on, safely stored in sub-conscious treasure
houses, ready to be evoked at will for the
refreshment of our spirits in hours of dearth

or gloom. Summer sunrise seen for the first time in the high Alps, the Sphinx looking out across the shimmering desert, the great Statue of Liberty greeting our first approach to the New World—best of all, perhaps, that marvellous transformation scene out of the noise and squalor of the railway station at Venice into a silent gondola gliding along mysterious canals—these stand out amongst " remembered joys ; store them up against the lean years ! "

Venice is no longer that unravished bride of quietness, as in the days when Turner saw visions and Ruskin dreamed dreams there. The Lido with its brilliant crowds of cosmopolitan holiday makers, its extravagant hotels and fashionable frivolities, has in some measure troubled the serene and romantic atmosphere of the city, arousing wrath and contempt in the bosom of its Intelligentsia.

> " For alas ! it is seldom, if ever,
> That people behave as they should ;
> For the Good *are* so harsh to the Clever,
> And the Clever *so* rude to the Good."

61

KITCHEN ESSAYS

Perhaps the slight moral relaxation that so insidiously steals over almost everybody on their Venetian holiday is one of its subtlest charms, and that it was indeed here that the lady in the story received a proposal of marriage over the telephone, and at once replied : " Yes, delighted ; but who is it ? "

The more vivid experiences of life in Venice can hardly fade even from the most sluggish or frivolous minds, being what the furniture dealer superfluously described as " so *very* unique." That first passing out of the glittering beauty of the Piazza into the subdued splendour of St. Mark's, that last sunset behind the Alps watched from San Giorgio's high belfry, the mellow fruitfulness of the heaped barges unloading their piles of gourds and grapes, of pomegranates, figs, and tomatoes, to the sound of morning church bells clanging out across the Rialto—these are memories to cherish and revive, lest life disallow the desired encore. And, as taste and smell are said to recall past impressions more vividly than written words, let us conjure up a Venetian dish or two, enjoying our *collazione* under an imagined pergola, with the sunlight playing through the leaves, the orange sails flapping idly in the calm air of the lagunes, or it may be with a rising moon and the gay allurement of Japanese lanterns twinkling on phosphorescent water, whilst mandolines and singing voices vibrate joyously through the darkness.

Certain specially Venetian products cannot be transplanted: *Uove fragole*, those strange little slimy grapes with their evasive flavour of mountain strawberry; *scampi*, those glorified prawns from the outer waters; *beccafichi*, poor tiny finches who feed on gaping figs, and whose innocent lives were ever pleaded for in vain; vine-fattened *escargi* like giant snails; strange, repellent *fruta di mare*, *nespoli*, *pomidoro*, *marinelli*, *polenta*, *funghi*, *poppone*. Their names are richly reminiscent, but their emigration overseas impossible—nay, undesirable. But *Minestra*, *Gnocchi con formaggio*, *Fritto Misto*,

63

Zabaione—these can all be summoned out of the magician's oven. And this is how it can be done.

Minestra. (*Vegetable Soup.*)

Take 4 fine tomatoes, 2 onions, a head of celery (white part only). Season well and cut into dice. Simmer in 2 oz. butter for about 20 minutes without colouring them. Add 1 quart good stock, preferably veal, 1 tablespoonful vermicelli. Simmer all for 30 minutes, taking off any scum. Just before serving in a marmite pot add a small pinch of sugar.

Gnocchi con formaggio.

Half a pint of milk, ½ lb. flour, ¼ lb. butter, 6 eggs, ¼ lb. grated cheese, salt, pepper. Boil the milk and butter, sift in the flour, stirring with wooden spoon, add eggs one by one, lastly cheese. Put this paste into a bag with a forcing pipe and squeeze it out, cutting off small pieces into a saucepan of boiling salted water. Poach for 10 minutes, drain, lay in flat fireproof dish, adding liberally some white sauce, some cream and grated cheese. Put into oven for 20 to 25 minutes, serving very hot and slightly browned.

Fritto Misto.

Half a pound calf's liver, ½ lb. veal cutlet, 1 sweetbread or some lamb's breads, 2 kidneys, 1 set of brains, 1 aubergine or artichoke, 1 cauliflower. Blanch the cauliflower, thoroughly cleanse and press the sweetbreads and brains, cut all into thin slices, season, dip in warm butter, and flour twice. *Sauté* these in separate pans in liberal butter, and serve straight from fire in hot dish, adding the juice of a lemon to the butter, and straining it on to the assembled parts. Garnish with quarters of lemon. These ingredients could be served crisply fried in oil if preferred instead of cooked in a *sauté* pan, but the first is a more savoury luncheon dish.

Zabaione. (A Venetian sweet to be served in six pretty tall coloured hock or long glasses.)

Break the yolks only of 6 fresh eggs into a *bain-marie*. In another pan make a thin syrup of 8 lumps of sugar soaked in a large tablespoonful of Marsala or any wine preferred, boil quickly and pour on the yolks slowly, whisking all over a pan of boiling water for about 10 minutes whilst it thickens and rises. Serve immediately in glasses previously well warmed, and send round with thin slices of sponge cake dried and crisped in the oven.

IX

HOME THOUGHTS OF FLORENCE AND SOME TUSCAN RECIPES

To tax and to please, like to love and to be wise, is not given to man, wrote Burke, that incomparable artist in the concise expression of great truths, and those who have suffered under the burdens of taxation since the Great War, and experienced the increasing difficulty of adjusting income to expenditure, are apt to think that life is less difficult in the sunny south than under grey English skies. To impoverished poets, artists, and writers, to all those with more past than present, Florence has ever offered the treasures of her beauty, of her sunshine and flowers, at moderate cost and with generous hands ; and though ninepence for fourpence is not really easier to find there than at home, it may often take the hopeful wanderer some time to discover this truth. Two such wanderers, having come thus far, decided that it was useless to indulge in vain regrets, for " the gods were right when they forbade Orpheus to look behind." Better far to enjoy the delights proffered so freely on all sides, and to forget for a while, if possible, the sordid limitations of a reduced income.

One of the economists varied her Mornings in Florence at the shrines of Giotto and Fra Angelico, of Botticelli and Michael Angelo, with others spent in a delightful " *cucinetta* " under the guidance of a smiling adept, who revealed the mysteries of Pasti and Legumi, of Minestrone and Frittura, of Insalata and Dolce, with obliging charm.

There is no hunger like that engendered in picture galleries, no fatigue comparable to that of the conscientious sightseer after prolonged contemplation of the world's masterpieces. Let us recapture, if may be, some of those simple Tuscan dishes offered to exhausted culture in exile, but equally enjoyable whether there or here.

SOME TUSCAN RECIPES

First let us, like the cheerful windmills bickering across the valleys in R. L. Stevenson's earliest journey to the Lowlands, engage ourselves " in the happy occupation of making bread." Not that bitter bread of exile known to the poet, but that agreeable form called *Panettone*, so greatly enjoyed by Mr. and Mrs. Robert Browning at sunny breakfasts in Casa Guidi. And if you wish to be truly Florentine, you will also learn to make, and like, *Gressini*, which can keep a hungry man nibbling patiently whilst the *Polenta* or the *Risotto* of his choice takes on the finishing touches preparatory to its savoury advent, heralded by the encouraging prelude : " Restono serviti, Signori, buon pranzo ! "

Panettone.

One pound of flour, ½ lb. butter or less, ¼ lb. sugar, ¼ lb. raisins, 3 eggs, lemon peel grated, ½ oz. of baker's yeast. Mix flour overnight with a little water and some baker's yeast in a basin with 1 egg and a little butter to form a not very stiff paste. Cover with a cloth and stand in a warm place all night to rise. In the morning, when it should have risen well, add remaining butter, dissolve the 2 eggs, sugar, peel, and raisins. Mix to medium consistency, and make this into a round roughly moulded flat loaf. If the dough is not stiff enough to keep in shape confine within a metal ring some 9 inches across, and bake until it has doubled its size in a moderate oven. Then make a large cross on it, brush with white of egg, sprinkle with pounded sugar and scraps of butter, and finish in a quick oven.

Gressini.

Half a pound of flour and pinch of salt, $\frac{1}{2}$ oz. butter, saltspoonful baking powder. Put these in a basin and mix with boiling water, not very moist. Then turn out and knead well until quite smooth, and roll with hands into sticks about the thickness of a cedar pencil, and some 9 or 10 inches long. Bake in a moderate oven till quite hard throughout, which takes a long time. They should be crisp and biscuit-coloured, and are served in dozens, with bread, in baskets abroad.

SOME TUSCAN RECIPES

Polenta au Gratin.

Into a pint of boiling water (salted) pour
about a breakfast cup of polenta, or
maize flour, stir well, boil for 25 minutes,
add 2 oz. butter and some 2 oz. of
parmesan cheese. Spread this on a
buttered baking sheet. When cold cut
into rounds the size of a wine glass ;
brown the rounds of polenta in butter
each side in a frying-pan, lay them just
overlapping in a buttered fireproof dish,
with grated parmesan and nut-brown
butter poured over, and finish in the
oven. Serve very hot. If preferred, a
creamy cheesy sauce can be poured
over the polenta rounds and put into
the oven to brown.

Risotto.

Put into a stewpan 1 pint good stock,
preferably veal, ¼ lb. rice (Italian
the best). Cook slowly with a pinch of
saffron tied in muslin, to be removed
when rice is cooked. Take a small
onion cut into dice and fry in butter,
also a couple of skinned tomatoes, or
some mushrooms cut in slices and fried,
and ¼ lb. grated parmesan. Add all
these to the rice with a walnut-sized

71

piece of butter, stirring all carefully together, and salt to taste. If too stiff add a little more stock. Scraps of white chicken cut in shreds, or their livers fried in butter, can be placed on the top of the risotto. The Milanese add beef marrow and white wine; the Neapolitans season with pounded prawns and garnish with lobster. Fragments of pork or of truffles can be brought to the service of this dish, whose infinite variety need never stale with custom.

Mont Blanc.

Italians are fond of sweets, but unimaginative in their preparation. Here is a delicious one, for which the chestnuts of Vallombrosa yearly patter to the ground in their thousands. Take of them, roasted and peeled, 1 lb., and put in a stewpan with vanilla pod, $\frac{1}{4}$ lb. sugar, a little milk, $\frac{1}{4}$ lb. of best chocolate. Cook till soft. Rub through coarse sieve into a basin-shaped mould well sprinkled with grated chocolate. Turn out, and mask to whiteness with thinly whipped sweetened cream. Serve cold on a silver dish.

X

SOME BREAKFAST-TIME SUGGESTIONS.—I

BREAKFAST is the most difficult meal of the day, whether from its social or its culinary aspect. Many of us feel like that man who, meeting a bore, said, " If you have got anything to say to me I wish you would kindly say it to somebody else." Our reluctant consciousness, but newly returned from a dream world, shrinks from all but the gentlest contacts. " Praise me not too much," as Odysseus said to Diomed, " neither find fault with me at all," and the greetings of melancholic and dissatisfied individuals can, like the cry of the curlew in Miss Barlow's Irish idyll, set our whole mental landscape into a minor key for the rest of the day.

Not that we may permit ourselves too

churlish a licence, as did that misanthrope asked by his talkative barber how he would wish his hair cut. " In perfect silence," came the discouraging reply ! Fortunately there are some rare companionships which never come amiss, and their presence, even at the breakfast table, breeds perpetual benediction—some bright spirits who can irradiate the gloom of the most cheerless morning, even as " the lark who meets the rain halfway and sings it down."

A *cordonbleu* cannot be at her best very early in the day ; and as for a chef, he will unblushingly delegate his duties to his understudy. It is wise, therefore, to aim at simplicity, but, within its limits, to strive after perfection. Above all things, breakfast must be hot, and many breakfasters resemble Belconan the West Indian, who said of himself : " No one sins with more repentance, or repents with less amendment, than do I." That long metal food-warmer with spirit lamps known as " the Sluggard's Delight," whereon porridge, coffee, and hot dishes

can be kept palatable, is a great help. Insist
on a hot-water kettle of real efficiency, on a
tea-caddy which will contain a delicate as
well as a pungent blend of tea, more than
one tea-pot, and a small saucepan over a
spirit lamp for boiling eggs, with an hour-
glass standing sentry near by. Readers
of Jane Austen will remember Serle's un-
rivalled success in this minor art, and can
emulate his skill. The French prefer eggs
boiled in water rising from warm to boiling,
instead of rushing them through by our rapid
three minutes' process. But this claims, perhaps, overmuch attention from a busy hostess.
Good coffee may come from Arabia or India,
from the Blue Mountains of Jamaica, or *via*
France with an admixture of chicory ; but
its flavour and excellence will be derived
from daily careful roasting and grinding,
a truism universally admitted and habitually
disregarded. A fireproof jug of ample pro-
portions with wide ventilated top should
keep the milk hot without boiling over ; and
if you can persuade your kitchen to follow

what used to be a universal practice in the northern coffee-drinking countries, the day will begin pleasantly for you.

Frothed Coffee.

> Take 2 large tablespoonfuls of cream and froth it well with an egg-whisk, and pour it on the top of the hot milk just before serving. Each cup will get some of the foaming milk and both look and taste the nicer; and for a thin or specially deserving individual a spoonful can be surreptitiously skimmed off to cream a favoured cup. Having experienced this, you will not again sit down under the thick yellow blanket of scum which embarrasses all and disgusts many.

Toast, to be good, demands a glowing grate, a handy toasting-fork, and a patient watcher—counsels of perfection indeed, for the ideal rack is like friendship and the immortality of the soul, almost too good to be true. An anxious bride, humiliated by the sort of toast only a starving sparrow could relish, wrote to one learned in such matters, asking for a trustworthy recipe. " Cut a slice of bread, hold it before the fire, and say incantations," was the unhelpful but only advice vouchsafed. An electric griller can be used successfully by those who can successfully use such contraptions, but the elemental toasting - fork, the patient watcher before the fire, and a go-between, with the honour of the house at heart, are really the truest solution.

Here is a tried recipe for *Brioches*, very popular last summer on a big steam yacht, and worth the little trouble and practice required, especially for those of Continental breakfast habits.

Take $\frac{1}{2}$ lb. flour, less than $\frac{1}{2}$ lb. butter, 1 oz. sugar, pinch of salt, 3 eggs, $\frac{1}{2}$ oz. baker's yeast. Weigh the flour and put one quarter of it in a basin with sufficient tepid milk to mix into a light dough. Put aside to rise for ten minutes. Put the rest of the flour into a basin, make a hole for sugar, eggs, and salt beaten together, and now mix in the butter lightly. When this sponge is ready, add to it the smaller quantity of flour with yeast, knead, and leave in a cool place. Next morning form into small cakes of cottage-loaf shape, the lower part as big round as a claret glass, the upper of sherry-glass size, and bake. This quantity will make twelve brioches.

Here is a popular *Marmalade*, that first necessity of the Englishman's breakfast-table, which so perplexed the French commissariat in 1914.

Cut 13 selected Seville oranges into thin slices, removing only the pips; pour 6 quarts of water on, and let it stand 24 hours. Empty all into the preserving pan and boil slowly for 2 hours. Add 10 lb. loaf sugar, and boil up again for 1 hour. Just before taking off add the juice of 2 lemons. If the preserve is required dark and thick, the rind of the oranges should be scraped before slicing them and added with the sugar.

XI

SOME BREAKFAST-TIME SUGGESTIONS.—II

THE difficulties of the communal breakfast table having been lightly indicated in the preceding chapter, it remains still to consider what further avenues to success might be explored, if that hated phrase can be forgiven, remembering that " Where there is a will there is a way," truest of all proverbs, except perhaps that " Necessity is the mother of invention."

Having, then, indulged the late comers with ideal coffee, tea of preferred blend, freshly-made toast, perfectly boiled eggs, delicious fancy bread, and home-made marmalade, let us consider how best to comfort those early birds, the bread-winners, school folk, hunters, and sportsmen, who are apt by their premature descent and impatient bell-ringing to disturb the morning harmony of the home. There is nothing like Work, as Mr. Bernard Shaw reminds us (or was it Play ?), to make a man or woman really selfish. But with that excellent pacificator, a *Home-cured Tongue*, danger can be temporarily averted and appetite allayed. And here is the recipe from an old-fashioned country house, renowned for its successful preparation. Once experienced, it will be in perpetual session, " by request," on the sideboard, and no understudies in glasses or rolled, out of tins, can supplant this genuine article.

Of common salt 2 lb., of bay salt 1 lb., of saltpetre $\frac{1}{4}$ lb., and $1\frac{1}{2}$ lb. black treacle. Finely pound the salts and mix with the treacle. Choose two large fresh ox-tongues and rub them well with this mixture, turning them every day in their pickling bath for from 3 to 4 weeks, and letting them lie in the pickle. To be smoked for 2 days in a wood-fire chimney before boiling, and steeping with abundant vegetables and herbs, a few cloves and peppercorns, garnished with home-made glaze and a little aspic jelly. The result will repay the trouble, although unfairly, for ever one sows and another reaps.

Nowadays breakfast-table providers are so intimidated by the cost of first-rate *Hams* that they forbear to venture on any. Let them take courage, and see how good even an inexpensive one can be for human nature's daily food, if it be soaked for from twenty-four to forty-eight hours (according to size), slowly boiled for four hours, and when cold liberally strewed with that dark moist sugar known to the trade as Muscovado, browned with a red-hot salamander, and left to harden.

Of course a really first-rate ham, such as the peach-fed Spanish variety, or those excellent but costly brands from Yorkshire, Bradenham, or Cumberland, deserve special treatment in their boiling, such as a bottle of madeira and the addition of vegetables, spices, and herbs. Thus enriched, they should make ceremonial début at a luncheon or dinner-table, accompanied by Cumberland sauce and a skilfully composed salad before appearing at the breakfast sideboard.

At those seasons when tomatoes abound and rashers are dear, a dish called *Chasse* may be welcomed.

> Collect 1 onion, 6 tomatoes, 3 potatoes, a slice of ham, some grated cheese, red pepper, and a pinch of allspice. Fry the onion lightly, add the skinned tomatoes and ham, both cut up small. When these are well browned in a buttered *sauté* pan, add a little water and the diced potatoes, and cook slowly till these are done. Before serving mix in grated cheese slightly flavoured with red pepper till the mixture is ropy. Pour on a hot dish, and serve with nicely poached eggs on the top. If preferred, omit the cheese.

The old familiar breakfast dishes, porridge, eggs, bacon, fish (fresh and salted), kedgeree (dry or moist, curried or diversified with smoked haddock, sardine, or minced anchovy), omelets (plain or enfolding kidneys, mushrooms, tomatoes, or other savoury fillings), these will always hold their own on our conservative and often monotonous tables. Devonshire cream or potted shrimps may give a welcome touch of variety, and *American Cereals*, such as post-toasties, honey-grains, puffed wheat, or puffed rice, with or without cream, and fruits, fresh in summer, cooked in winter, could be used by young and old more plentifully than they are. Try reinforcing, and thereby economizing, your crisply curled best *Breakfast Bacon* with an abundant admixture of yesterday's potatoes, cut in cubes, tossed in bacon fat, and served piping hot. Try *Bananas* skinned and halved across, and again lengthwise, and served frizzling from a buttered *sauté* pan on fried toast, with perhaps a dash of orange juice added, an excellent and wholesome food for the young. The delicate or elusive guest who breakfasts upstairs in happy *tête-à-tête* with early post and morning papers, will enjoy a slice of melon or half a *Grape-Fruit*, daintily prepared and served very cold and juicy in its own skin. *French Plums*, stoned and stewed to softness, *Apples* baked or made into an appetizing brown purée, with but a tinge of sugar and a flavouring of lemon rind—these are wholesomer for the sedentary than animal foods, and should give welcome variety. Indeed, apples are proverbially so health-giving that no doctors can be expected to do anything but eat them themselves and discourage that practice in others, especially during an abundance of that unexcelled variety, Cox's Orange Pippin. It is true that in the Oriental legend, Azrael, the Angel of Death, accomplished his mission by holding to the nostril an apple from the Tree of Life; but the story is figurative and the meaning mystical.

How good the old-fashioned Scotch breakfasts used to be, and how hospitable their welcome to the Highlands at Perth Station or on a West Coast steamer! Here is a recipe for *Scotch Scones*, also one for *Quince Jelly*, both from a northern stillroom, birthplace of many remembered good things.

BREAKFAST-TIME SUGGESTIONS

To about ½ lb. flour add a pinch of salt, ¼ teaspoonful of carbonate of soda, and ½ teaspoonful cream of tartar, and mix. Rub into the flour a walnut-sized piece of butter, and with some butter-milk, or sour milk, make into a moist dough. Roll out, and cut into small rounds if for breakfast, or larger three-cornered shapes if for school-room tea, and place on a girdle made hot and sprinkled with flour. Bake till each side is a pale brown. A trifle of sugar can be added to the flour if sweetened scones are preferred.

Quince Jelly.

Peel and cut up the quinces into quarters, and put into a preserving pan with enough water to cover them. Simmer until soft and of a pale pink colour, and the water reduced. Strain through a hair sieve or fine cloth into a basin. Allow 1 lb. of sugar to 1 pint of juice. Boil the juice for 20 minutes before adding the sugar, and boiling all together, removing scum as it rises, for some 20 minutes, or until it jellies when tried on a plate. It should be a nice red colour, and poured into small-sized white jars and covered tight from air.

Put these suggestions, incomplete though they be, into the household kitchen book, establishing thereby a worthy tradition, for the day will come when, in the words of a contemporary humorist, it will be said regretfully, " She was a good cook as cooks go . . . and as cooks go, she went." Nevertheless the law of the kitchen should remain, and at a breakfast table thus furnished, " Good morning " will not be a perfunctory greeting or merely a pious wish, but the assured prelude to a good day.

XII

TEA-TIME AND SOME CAKES

Two divergent schools of thought contend
round the tea table, the one belittling its
importance, the other exaggerating its opportunities. They urge opposing points of
view, often with an acerbity out of keeping with its temperate hospitality. Sydney
Smith was moved to fervent piety as he
poured out his third cup, " thanking Heaven
that he had not been born before the coming-
in of tea "; and readers of Scott will remember in *St. Ronan's Well* the vehemence with
which Meg Dods repelled Captain Mac-
Turk's base insinuation : " Me drunk, you
scandalous blackguard ! " she cried, waving
her tempestuous broomstick, " me that am
fasting from all but sin and bohea."

Of late the medical profession, reinforced

87

by Fashion and Sport, both calling out for
slimness and muscle in their respective
votaries, has conspired against the sociable
rite with its insidious accompaniments.
" What ! " they say, shaking a forbidding
finger in their costly confessionals, " two
cups of tea a day, my dear sir (or madam) !
No wonder that you are ill ! " " Le fiv'-
o'-clock " has in recent years established
itself abroad, and we shall continue no doubt
to enjoy its indulgences in spite of the slight
sense of guilt which accompanies and possibly enhances their practice.

For the generation now passing away, tea
was only clandestinely procurable by joining
the children, and still it seems to have a
special charm out of nursery mugs with hot
toast made and buttered over the high fender
as only Nurse knows how to do it, or shared
on the schoolroom hearthrug surrounded
by jam-eating clamorous youth, when it
tastes so much better than on the gilt chairs
accompanied by decorous drawing-room
conversation.

88

TEA-TIME AND SOME CAKES

During the war years even the office yielded to the allurements of afternoon tea, and the humours of its preparation by flappers, and its enjoyment by their principals, provided the caricaturist and the letter-writer to the papers with much happy inspiration and spiteful suggestion.

Hungry hunters and shooters, triumphant and bemired from the chase, love to quench their thirst and spoil their dinners under the stuffed heads in the great hall, and golfers and fishermen to magnify their exploits amid the miscellaneous companionship of the hotel lounge. All these confess the hour with grateful pleasure, but the true spiritual home of the tea-pot is surely in a softly-lighted room, between a deep arm-chair and a sofa cushioned with Asiatic charm, two cups only, and these of thinnest china, awaiting their fragrant infusion, whilst the clock points nearer to six than five, and a wood fire flickers sympathetically on the hearth.

George Herbert, in his poem beginning

" Content thee, greedie heart ! " reminds us with superfluous cruelty that we cannot " both eat our cake and have it," and though to try is as human as to fail, we should at least ascertain what our cake is made of and weigh carefully all its ingredients before deciding which we will do with it. Here is one called *Caraway Tea Bread* baked specially for the Nursery, which grown-ups will do well to visit on its afternoon début. Ingredients :

> Three teacups of flour, 2 teaspoonfuls baking powder, 1 teacup castor sugar, 1 large dessertspoonful ground caraway seeds, 1 egg, 3 oz. butter, 1 teacupful of boiling milk. Mix flour, baking powder, and sugar, rub in butter, mix the milk warmed with the egg beaten and the ground caraway seeds. Knead into a flattish brick-shaped loaf or cake, and bake 20 minutes in a quick oven. To be eaten fresh, with a little butter.

For the hungry Schoolroom, when friends come to tea, here is an excellent *Stollen Cake*, and if treated more lavishly in the matter of candied peel and raisins, there is no board it might not suitably adorn.

One pound flour ($\frac{1}{2}$ lb. extra for kneading in), 5 oz. stoned raisins, 4 oz. currants, 4 oz. butter, 4 oz. sugar, 2 eggs, 2 oz. baker's yeast. Pour a little lukewarm milk over the yeast, mix the warmed flour with a little milk, add yeast, and mix. Place the dough in a warm place to rise for an hour. Mix in the melted butter, eggs, sugar, fruit, grated peel of a lemon, and some candied peel, and knead well with remaining flour. Put back to rise for 1 hour. Place the dough on a baking sheet, making it into an oval flat shape, fold one side half over, brush with egg, strew with halved almonds and sugar. Bake 45 minutes in a hot oven. Sprinkle with icing sugar when baked.

Here is something for the dyspeptic guest who never eats anything at tea, followed by something for the robuster one who occasionally eats too much.

Brown Flour Biscuits.

Half a pound brown flour, 6 oz. butter, a pinch of baking powder, another of salt. Rub together, mix with milk, roll out thin, cut in wine-glass-sized rounds. Bake 5 minutes in a hot oven.

For a festive occasion try this :—

Super-Chocolate Cake.

Half a pound fresh butter beaten to a cream, 7 eggs (yolks and whites beaten separately, and the whites stirred in the last thing), ½ lb. best vanilla chocolate grated and heated in oven, then beaten up in the butter with 3 oz. dried flour, ¼ lb. sifted sugar, 4 oz. ground almonds, 1 teaspoonful of sal volatile. Bake in a slack oven, then ice with thin soft icing flavoured with maraschino. If ingredients are thoroughly beaten up it will be very light.

Lest this last calls for a reproach from the thrifty, here is a nice useful cake suited to the Rector's 5 o'clock call, or the ladies of the local political organization in conclave, and good for the office luncheon tin or the fisherman's basket next day.

Wardley Cake.

Half a pound ground rice, ½ lb. flour, ½ lb. butter, ½ lb. castor sugar, ½ lb.

crystallized or glacé ginger, a few glacé
cherries, ½ pint milk, ½ teaspoonful
bicarbonate of soda. Warm the butter
and milk, and add them to dry ingredients, mixing well. Bake at once for
from 2½ to 3 hours.

As a final suggestion, here is a sand-cake
for a syren's tea-party of two. It was known
in the Vienna of happier days as a *Venus
Torte*, and might be served with honey-dew
and the milk of Paradise when procurable.

Clarify 1 lb. butter. When cold beat to
a cream, add 12 oz. sugar, 1 lb. potato
flour (sieved), 4 whole eggs and the
yolks of two, the zest of 1 lemon. Beat
the whole mass for 1 hour, when it
should form bubbles. Bake in a buttered
and finely bread-crumbed mould in a
moderate oven. Halve these quantities
for a small cake.

XIII

A LITTLE DINNER BEFORE
THE PLAY

ONE of the compensations of an annual
return to the city after summer holidays
and to the more serious life of the winter
months is to be found in the wealth of good
things offered for our improvement and
relaxation as the long evenings close in.
In the words of Mr. Kipling :—

"Bar home the door of summer nights
   Lest those high planets drown
The memory of near delights
   In all the longed-for town."

One of these near delights is assuredly
a good play in congenial company after a
pleasant dinner. This, to be successful,
must be planned with care, and neither
timed so late as to produce hurry and conse-

94

quent irritation, nor so early as to discon-
cert the busy and encourage the unpunctual.
The table must not be served with too many
good things, lest they induce lethargy, nor
yet must the tired worker arise hungry and
unrefreshed. A course of *Soup and Fish
combined*, one satisfying meat or game dish,
with vegetables and salad, another merging
sweet and dessert into one—this will be more
acceptable to eager play-goers as well as more
considerate to any elders of sensitive digestion and leisurely habit than the customary
more protracted meal, and should admit
of perfect and unruffled service.

Souchet of Slips.

Allow one slip for each person, skin and
trim off sides and head, put the trimmings into enough good stock for number required, add some vegetables, and
let simmer gently for 2 or 3 hours.
Strain and clarify in the usual way for
consommé. Prepare a julienne of
carrots, turnips, and leeks. Add these
when cooked to the cleared soup, and
simmer altogether for half an hour or

so, the slips meanwhile to be placed in a fireproof dish and poached in salted water. When ready to serve, boil up soup, pour into a hot tureen, adding the slips drained from their water, and serve together in soup plates, with horse-radish-cream sauce, and brown bread and butter going round at once with it.

Côtelettes en Robes de Chambre.

Take selected lamb or mutton cutlets. Grill them lightly and leave to get cold. Take some good gravy stock and mix in a little tomato purée. Add fine cut ham or tongue, or both. Spread some of this thickened sauce on to each cutlet, and wrap them round with a jacket of lightly-made puff-pastry. Cook them in a brisk oven till nicely browned, and serve very hot on a long, narrow dish, accompanied by the same sauce, only less thick, in a sauce-boat and by a pile of French beans, or peas, "à la crème," sharing another long dish with a *Purée of Mashed Potatoes*, not that stiff and tasteless compound so often offered, but the French variety made by boiling and draining the potatoes, and then

96

mashing them in a saucepan lightly rubbed with a clove of garlic, and mixed with a liberal amount of butter, and either boiling milk, or, as some cooks prefer, with a little stock from the soup-pot, which makes it a little browner; and this need be hardly thicker than a well-made apple sauce. Another method would be to boil a Portuguese onion very soft, and beat it hot with four times its weight in potatoes, adding cream, butter, pepper, the yolks of 2 eggs, and salt, and pass through a sieve. Make this mixture into round golf balls, and flavour with salt, pepper, and chopped parsley, brush with egg and fine stale crumbs, and brown in the oven on a buttered tin, and serve on the same dish as the green vegetables.

If lighter nourishment be preferred, a fat *Quail* cooked and served inside a puff-pastry jacket, the legs just peeping out, should emerge moist but done to a turn, and accompanied by a salad of blanched endive surrounding a sparely sweetened compote of Russian cranberry. Or, as an alternative suggestion, choose *Bécassines Flambées* (Snipe on Fire), a bird to each guest, to appear on a silver or metal dish, perfectly roasted, and sitting each on a toast lightly fried and spread with the liver, etc., well pounded. Outside the serving door let a couple of tablespoonfuls of brandy, previously warmed in a small casserole over a spirit lamp, be set alight and poured flaming over and around the birds just as they come to the table. Crisp potato straws or thin fried rounds of Jerusalem artichoke and a salad of celery shredded and enriched by cream, and surrounded with watercress or lamb's lettuce, should accompany this dish.

To combine the sweet and dessert courses into one, a fruit dish seems desirable, and a nice looking *Pine-apple* with a decorative top might be chosen, the upper end sliced off so as to give an adequate opening by which to scoop out the fruit and juice and make of them a delicious cream or water ice as preferred, in the approved manner, and this can be served inside the pine-apple standing upright, its top being replaced for its first introduction to the party. With this, send round an ample shallow cake covered with soft icing, well flavoured with maraschino and decorated with glacé cherries or some preserved cubes of pine-apple cut in half. If liked, the cake might have a layer of soft icing inside as well. An alternative suggestion, if ice is not desired or pine-apples are too expensive that day, might be to choose some large seedless juicy oranges, one for each guest, removing the top and with it an inch or more of the fruit, which must be all scooped out, cut and shredded small, and returned to the lower and larger half of the orange, minus pith or · pip, and plus a syrup of the juice enriched with curaçoa or sherry. A thin méringue mixture, replacing their own top halves, and lightly coloured in a quick oven, then left to cool, will bonnet them attractively, and a short sojourn in the ice-box give them a refreshing chill. With these might come in a flat sponge, or similar cake, flavoured with orange-flower water, and roofed over with a soft icing—this also orange-flavoured with rasped rind, and decorated with candied orange rings cut up.

There should still be time for a perfect cup of coffee and a possible liqueur, and, most desired of all by many, for a good *smoke*, without which there will be no social fire. Warmed thus and fed, the play-goers will be attuned to enjoyment and ready to appreciate each other, their dinner, their play, and their hostess, " and so to bed with great contentment."

XIV

A LITTLE SUPPER AFTER THE PLAY

THERE is a sharp cleavage of opinion between the pleasure-seekers who prefer a reinforced tea or a stirrup-cup of soup and a sandwich before an evening's entertainment, with prospect of supper to come, and those who will have the accustomed meal at 6, 7, or 8, and "won't wait." The hour when the play begins, the claims of the working day, and the locality of the home are the deciding factors. The restaurant has its drawbacks, and those are fortunate who can command, especially in winter, a pleasant meal by their own firesides, with no anxiety in the matter of procurable drinks, no waiting for disengaged tables, no apprehension as to adequate ready money for that unknown quantity, the bill, that embarrassing problem, the tips. Few households can cope with the preparation of a hot meal late at night, except as a very occasional dissipation, but with one servant in attendance there should be no difficulty in arranging for a good supper with a marmite of soup kept hot on a metal food warmer or spirit lamp. This recipe is a comforting one, and suitable for a chilly night :—

Consommé à la Indienne, for six persons.

Put into a stewpan a quart of good stock, slice into it 2 onions, 1 large cooking apple, a tablespoonful of desiccated cocoanut, a dessertspoonful of curry powder (or more if it is liked hot), and the carcass of a roast chicken, rabbit or game bones, and let simmer gently for an hour. Strain and remove the fat, and clarify in the usual manner. Re-boil and serve with pieces of game or chicken in the marmite, and a very little plain boiled rice, also kept hot, to be added into each portion as helped.

A long dish of oysters is universally popular with men, but the oysters must

have first-class references and be freshly
opened, and served very cold, with brown
bread and butter, red pepper, lemon quarters, white vinegar handy. Women often
find it more blessed to give than to receive
their proportion of 4 to the male 6, and these
are perhaps easier to have very good at a
first-rate restaurant or oyster bar than at
home late in the evening. A good alternative is a cold *Soufflé of Lobster*, prepared
and served up just before the cook goes to
bed. This recipe is excellent also for summer
luncheon parties, or as an extra course at
dinner.

> Choose a lobster weighing a little over
> 1 lb. for six or eight guests. Take all the
> fish from the shell, saving fair slices of the
> best parts for decorating the top ; chop
> the remainder very fine, and mix with
> ¼ pint whipped cream, and season to
> taste. Pound the shell well, and add
> a little butter, and simmer on the fire
> with about 2 tablespoonfuls of milk.
> Strain through muslin, and add when
> cold to the cream and lobster. Melt
> about 4 leaves of gelatine and stir into

the lobster cream. Have ready a round white china or silver soufflé dish with crisp shredded lettuce, hard-boiled egg, bits of skinned tomato, a little thin mayonnaise sauce passed through it all, reaching half-way up the dish, and put above this foundation the mixture of lobster; and when set put over a thin layer of aspic jelly slightly pink with cochineal and the selected pieces of lobster, and serve very cold with bread and butter.

For the *pièce de résistance* try a *Chaud-froid de Volaille*, made with the best parts of 2 chickens, or 2 pheasants, or a small turkey. These should be cut up, after boiling, into fillets or neat helpings, and when cold enriched with a spreading from a tin of purée de foie gras, or the remains of a terrine; and if there are any truffle peelings available so much the better. Lay these fillets on a long silver or metal dish, mask them thinly with liquid aspic, with more finely-chopped aspic at the ends as a garnish. Between each fillet arrange upstanding sheaves of uncooked celery, finely cut and encouraged to curl so that it looks in shape like a shock of corn ready to be carried, and is white with cream well whipped and seasoned with salt and pepper and a drop of tarragon vinegar. Any other cold salad garnish of single lettuce leaves or small skinned tomatoes could embellish this dish.

The *Aspic Jelly*

> to be made with a pint of brown stock, adding a little carrot, onion, celery, parsley, and a few pimentoes (allspice), with a dessertspoonful of tarragon vinegar and a teaspoonful of Worcester sauce. About 8 leaves of gelatine and 2 whites of eggs whisked all together in a stew-pan. Place on stove and bring slowly to the boil. When clear, strain through a fine cloth into a basin and use as required.

For sweets nothing is nicer than this specially good *Orange Jelly*. Not that stiffly moulded, colourless, and acid variety so usually and deservedly rejected, but soft and shapeless, of the colour of a blood orange, and really tasting of the fruit, served in a large shallow glass dish, and accompanied by another dish containing a fresh *Compote of Oranges* made in the approved way, the fruit uncooked, all pith and pip removed, and a hot syrup of sugar and juice poured over the orange segments and allowed to cool.

Recipe for old-fashioned Orange Jelly.

Half a pound loaf sugar, 18 oranges, 2 lemons, 1 oz. gelatine. Boil the sugar to a syrup, pour it boiling hot on the thinly peeled rinds of 2 oranges. Squeeze the juice of all the oranges, pass through a silk sieve, add the dissolved gelatine and syrup and a few drops of cochineal, and serve in glass bowl not moulded. With this jelly and fruit have a plate of thin long *Caramel Biscuits* which are generally purchased at a costly confectioner's, but are not difficult to accomplish at home, given one in the kitchen who can make good pastry.

Make some light puff pastry and roll it out in castor sugar instead of flour, and cut it into long narrow shapes, some 6 to 8 inches long, and 2 to 3 inches wide. Bake in a medium oven very brown and crisp and blistered, and rather sticky, like brandy snaps.

A SUPPER AFTER THE PLAY

As regards supper drinks, it rests with the
host whether champagne or sparkling moselle,
white wine, whisky and soda, or temperance
drinks such as orangeade or dry ginger-ale
and cider mixed, be provided. The male
oyster-eater would welcome a glass of porter
with that course, whilst feminine taste would
go in the direction of Chablis. Some good
cigars and cigarettes, a bottle of liqueur, and
some sweets should not be forgotten, and
will promote the success of the evening.

Of course the prudent and far-seeing
would eat and drink none of these things :
they would partake of a cup of hot Benger
by their own bedsides. But, then, these
suggestions need never have been written,
and the evening would assuredly have ended
but tamely—" Eudaemonia (Happiness) is a
good daemon," said the Ancients, and a wise
poet of our own day (John Masefield) bids us—

"Best trust the happy moments—what they gave
Makes man less fearful of the certain grave,
And gives his work compassion and new eyes—
The days that make us happy make us wise."

P.S.—Don't forget some hot bovril and sandwiches for any motor-men waiting to take the guests home ; you will thereby be doing as you would be done by, and the supper-party will be the merrier and more prolonged.

XV

A WINTER SHOOTING-PARTY LUNCHEON

THE successful organization of a shooting-party luncheon away from home calls for forethought and preparation if the occasion is to be one of unruffled enjoyment, and some quiet staff work before the business of the week begins will lessen the strain on kitchen and pantry, already taxed by the requirements of a house party. " The fussed shall be last, and the last shall be fussed," as a wise old nurse was wont to observe soothingly to her charges, restive under the rival claims of cleanliness, punctuality, and pleasure.

It may probably be necessary to provide for some ten or twelve luncheon guests, as, given suitable conditions of weather, and place, the five or six guns will be joined by the women of the party, and there will be, in addition, keepers, beaters, and loaders. Beaters have large meat sandwiches and bread and cheese from the house, or they may, by arrangement considered in their pay, bring their own luncheon, the employer only providing beer. Keepers and loaders are also provided with cold luncheon, and it is convenient to put this into separate named packets, thereby utilizing varieties of cold meat, cake, or cheese, and simplifying the process of rapid distribution. A little consideration for those whose daily fare is often rough and meagre will be greatly appreciated, but the details of this branch of the commissariat are often best settled by the head keeper and cook in conclave, though the knowledge that it is of kindly concern to master and mistress will ensure suitable provision for all. George Sala was wont to tell of one who threw largesse in the face of the poor so rudely that it hurt them, and in their wrath they forbore to return thanks.

A SHOOTING-PARTY LUNCHEON

In those good old days people refer to regretfully, but are practically unwilling to recall, the hardy sportsman would make his frugal luncheon from the remains of the ample breakfast table, filling a roll with strange combinations of " left-overs " (as our American friends neatly call them), wrapping up a buttered scone with a slice of ham and a hard-boiled egg, adding a biscuit and a wedge of cheese, or perhaps only a piece of cake and an apple bulging his ample pockets. This iron age was succeeded by the extravagant times preceding the war, and it is for us to cherish still good habits of moderation. If game must be reared and then shot, at least let the shooting be sportsmanlike and the quantity moderate, and let not the precious gifts of fresh air and exercise be neutralized by over-elaborate feasting. " Good, but simple," should be the keynote.

The scene of the shooting luncheon should be for choice under cover in cold weather—a keeper's cottage, a farm-house parlour, a forester's lodge, or a conveniently placed

summer-house of wood and thatch, dedicated to such occasions, where necessary
equipment could be kept. Stores and camp
furnishers nowadays have a wide choice of
portable tables, benches, and camp-stools.
Roomy fireproof pots and dishes, with
covers, unbreakable plates and cups, nests
of metal or horn tumblers fitting into each
other, a wooden bowl for baked potatoes,
and large thermos flasks for hot coffee are
necessary. For those who don't possess
fitted luncheon baskets, two large rolls of
silver aeroplane cloth—one for knives, the
other for spoons and forks—will be found
convenient, and if divided up, bound and
tied with bright worsted braid, each article
can be readily slipped in and out of the
stitched-down divisions on their inner sides.
The same cloth, recently bought by many
when it glutted the market, would suitably
cover the table, and be easily sponged clean
and folded ; or a length of bright French
cotton check, with napkins to match, looks
nice : no dainty table linen or silver. Au-

tumn fern and beech leaves give a touch of beauty, or a gay basket, as made and dyed in many a local village industry, holding a bunch of spindleberry or butcher's broom, of forest evergreen or Christmas holly, is more " in the picture " than any more elaborate decorations.

Some suggestions, neither novel nor elaborate, since the occasion hardly calls for such, but possibly of use to hostess or cook beset by many conflicting claims, are offered. For the main dish a big brown marmite, piping hot from a hay-box, or warmed up on the cottage fire, the contents fresh neck of mutton or lamb, with potatoes and small pickling onions ; or, alternatively, a hotpot of game or poultry with celery, peeled chestnuts, and a milky gravy, flavoured with Worcester sauce or mushrooms, together with a bowl of jacketed potatoes and a casserole of baked beans. A good recipe for these and for a cold game pie is given, both always useful. Jam or spiced apple puffs, covered-in cheesecakes or mince-pies, are an easy second course to serve and consume; while a little truckle cheese or wedge of gruyère, with butter and lettuces or celery, and a tin of mixed plain biscuits hotted and served up crisp in their tin home, and a sportsman cake should be included. A brass dish of apples and pears makes the perfect centre-piece, and to comfort the chilly, slip in perhaps a box of dry Chinese ginger or some peppermint creams.

Shooters are thirsty folk, and will welcome a long draught of light beer, cider, or ginger ale; the old-fashioned may prefer claret or whisky with soda, and a modest flask of cherry brandy would be guiltily appreciated. Lock up the port till dinner-time, if good shooting be desired, but bring the cigars and cigarettes—the pipes will take care of themselves.

Cold Game Pie.

Take the flesh of a hare and cut into pieces the length of a finger; take the same weight of veal, or of chicken or pheasant mixed with veal, without fat or skin. Take 1½ lb. of sausage meat, and mix with the liver, etc., of the hare previously chopped small. Put pepper, salt, and a little thyme, and a bay leaf with a thin layer of stuffing at the bottom of a large earthenware game pie-dish. Put pieces of hare, veal, game, a slice of ham, a layer of stuffing, pressing the whole well down, no empty spaces left. Repeat till all meat is used, covering with a slice of ham or bacon, adding pepper, salt, thyme, and a bay leaf. Pour on the whole half a tumbler of water, 2 large tablespoonfuls of cognac. Close the terrine hermetically, pasting paper round the lid, and place in the oven for some 4 hours. Use cold.

Baked Beans.

Soak white or brown haricot beans overnight in cold water. In the morning cook in salted boiling water until tender. Drain, and put them in a deep fireproof dish with a cover. Add good tomato sauce, slightly thickened with flour and a little onion juice—or, if preferred, use soubise—stirring the sauce in with the beans and cooking in a slack oven, tightly covered, for 2 hours. Serve in the same dish.

Burnt House Cake.

Six oz. ground rice, 10 oz. flour, ½ lb. each of stoned raisins, sultanas, sugar, and butter. Beat butter to a cream with a 1d. packet of mixed spice. Dissolve 1 teaspoonful of bicarbonate of soda in ¼ pint of milk, which should be added to the other ingredients boiling hot, and baked in a moderate oven for an hour.

For some the best hour will come with the walk homewards in a gathering dusk, the winter sunset aflame in the west, and, as Dorothy Wordsworth puts it, " The country very solemn in the last hour of twilight ; it calls home the heart to quietness."

XVI

LUNCHEON FOR A MOTOR EXCURSION IN WINTER

" In justice to the ' Turk's Head,' it should be clearly stated that it does no more to cow and discourage travellers than many other provincial hotels in England," wrote a brilliant modern novelist lately; and a wit of the last century revenged himself for wrongs suffered, by the following impromptu written in a visitors' book at departure, and no doubt equally true to-day :—

"There stands an Inn below the hill, rightly named
'Pelican' from its enormous bill."

Similar experiences have suggested to many motorists of late that, until the innkeepers of " this dear, dear realm of England " emulate their foreign competitors in the provision of desirable food at reasonable cost, a home-made picnic may often prove the more excellent way. Tough joints, bluish rabbit or pork pies, fly-haunted ham bones, black-eyed potatoes, cheese rocky as its birthplace in lovely Cheddar, musty biscuits, indifferent bread and butter, an atmosphere redolent of stale tobacco and beer, attendants haughty, sometimes hostile, generally indifferent until tipping-time approaches—these are not rare and isolated exceptions, but the daily fare of our long-suffering race when they take the road.

Let us, then, get out the luncheon-basket from amongst the wedding presents of a richer age, and, in addition, contrive a small Norwegian kitchen or hay-box to hold a large screwed jar of comforting *Potage à la Écossaise*—meat, vegetables, and soup combined —a big thermos for *Mulled Claret*, and a smaller one for *Coffee*. Slip in a couple of camp-stools and a waterproof rug as well as our furs, so that we are not tied to the car or the roadside should some sheltered nook or sunny prospect allure us. Pour a moderately good bottle of claret into a saucepan, with half the rind of a lemon, 12 cloves, a pinch of nutmeg, a tablespoonful of sugar, and let these simmer, but not boil, serving very hot. Once experienced in perfection on a cold day it will not be forgotten, and should serve to warm and unstiffen the motorists without delay, whilst the luncheon is getting itself unpacked.

Potage à la Écossaise.

Put into rather more than a quart of good light stock some 2 tablespoonfuls of pearl barley (previously washed in cold water), a carrot, turnip, leek, onion, celery, a little cabbage or 3 or 4 Brussels sprouts, and let them cook gently together with the required number of nice cutlets from a well-selected and trimmed neck of mutton or lamb. Season with a little chopped parsley, cream, salt and pepper to taste, and a couple of teaspoonfuls of green peas, and some of those tiny new potatoes which the prudent housewife will have bottled like her gooseberries, or buried in a tin of dry sand for a winter luxury. The 6½d. Bazaar again sells charming quite small square or round white metal tins and nice horn or wooden spoons for the appropriate consumption of this dish.

Stuffed Salmon Rolls, for six persons.

First cook a slice of salmon (about ½ lb., and Norwegian might do), and when cold pass through a wire sieve and mix with a little mayonnaise sauce or whipped cream flavoured with a drop of Worcester sauce and tarragon vinegar. Add a pickled gherkin chopped small, and salt and pepper. Cut off the tops of the rolls or scones, remove the soft inside and butter them sparingly. Fill in with the prepared salmon, place a little shredded lettuce on top, and replace the lid with a thin slice of the buttered inside. A filling of egg and sardine, of minced chicken or game with cream and chopped walnut or beetroot, celery or gherkins, could be substituted, or some picked prawns or lobster with a little chopped aspic and salad.

For a *Winter Cake*, black and sticky with treacle, enlivened by whole white almonds, use this recipe :—

A MOTOR EXCURSION LUNCHEON

One pound of flour, 1 lb. black treacle,
1 dessertspoonful ground ginger, ½ lb.
brown sugar, ¼ lb. butter, ½ pint milk,
½ teaspoonful carbonate of soda, 4 eggs,
a little finely-chopped citron, and white
whole almonds for top. Mix the dry
ingredients together, warm the milk and
dissolve the butter in it, beat up the
eggs, then add treacle and stir into
the dry ingredients, beat well, bake ¾
hour. This mixture should be a running consistency before baking, so add
more milk if necessary. Bake in a flat
brick-shaped tin ; or if preferred round
and deep, a saucepan will serve.

Finally have a nice little selection for dessert instead of pudding, made up out of the
following suggestions. A small cream cheese
or Petit Suisse wrapped in a lettuce and some
crisp plain biscuits with a tiny pot of red
currant jelly (the combination so popular in
Duval restaurants), a box of fresh dates or
pulled figs, a carton of almonds and raisins,
or a little screw bottle of large black French
plums, or better still a basket of fresh fruit
costing what your purse can buy or your
fruit room produce, a handful of glacé

ginger cubes or a tin of peppermint creams, and lastly the cup of hot coffee, black or white, tasting as good out of the thermos as tea tastes nasty. And though there is no fire there can yet be smoke of cigarette, cigar, or pipe, to taste.

Now comes the moment for a gentle " promenade de digestion," or stretch across open country with a motor rendezvous at the end, for enjoying the scenery or local architecture, for taking intelligent interest in Roman camp or prehistoric remains, for noting the birds and sharing your food with them, for descending, like the prophet's ravens, with the surplus of your feast, on the nearest road-menders or country children, remembering to ask their acceptance thereof with all the courtesy you can command. Perhaps before you turn homewards you will collect a few delicate trails of ivy, better taken than left, from some wayside trees, to float in your flat bowl, or a bunch of late autumn foliage or winter evergreen to gladden your town home more intimately than florists' trophies. The nursery might be made happy by a sod of growing daisies from the hedgerow, such as have given great poets thoughts too deep for tears, and which could fill the empty luncheon receptacles, only forbearing to damage wild beauty which is everybody's possession. Such a day might well hold more material comfort and bodily invigoration, more imaginative suggestion as well as some saving to sorely-tried purses, than the hours often spent in stuffy public dining-rooms and crowded hotel lounges, for in the words of Meredith, " when we let Romance go, we change the sky for a ceiling."

XVII

COUNTRY FRIENDS TO A CHRIST-
MAS SHOPPING LUNCHEON

GOD made the first Christmas, and man has
ever since been busy spoiling it. Year by
year the propaganda of the shops grows in-
creasingly active; and their suggestions for
the keeping of that high feast, including such
secular items as dozens of brandy, whisky,
and champagne, appear annually more elaborate and incongruous than ever before. Experience leads us, however, to believe that
their lavish wares will all be sold and bought,
given and received, cherished or passed on,
as in the long tale of bygone years. Country
friends flock eagerly to town, armed with
lists of the things they are resolute to buy
and bestow, and the offer of a house of rest,
an hour of respite from their bewildering

A CHRISTMAS LUNCHEON

preoccupations, and an agreeable luncheon will be an act of hospitality gratefully welcomed. It will be the more appreciated if we take the trouble to order such fare as is not readily procurable in the country, for the charm of novelty is a potent one. " What is that delicious little cake ? " her late Majesty Queen Victoria is said to have inquired with interest, on being confronted for the first time with a penny bun. For a first course, then, choose a dish of oysters, rarely procurable at their best either at the seaside or in the country, serving them in their own half shells " au gratin," if not " au naturel."

Oysters au Gratin.

Choose the required number of plump native oysters, open, strain off the liquor, and beard them. Wash and dry the shells, butter their insides, shake over some fine stale bread-crumbs, and replace the oyster on a half shell. Cover it with more bread-crumbs, a little of its own liquor, a few grains of red or coralline pepper, a squeeze of lemon juice, and a very thin slice of fresh

125

butter. Bake 10 minutes in a hot oven, and brown with a salamander. Serve hot with brown bread, butter, and a garnish of parsley.

For an alternative, try this *Malay Curry of Prawns*, which should recapture the true Eastern flavour for a Western palate.

One cucumber, 1 cocoanut, and allow 4 prawns a head. 1. Remove shells from prawns, putting them into a *bain-marie*, and covering with milk to simmer for the sauce, placing prawns aside till required. 2. Peel and cut the cucumber into pieces like a large olive, boil in salted water, strain off and drain when cooked, but not overdone. 3. Drain the milk from cocoanut, retaining for use at the last, grate a cupful of the white part, pour over some boiling water, and let infuse. 4. Put in a stewpan a piece of butter, adding when melted a small onion cut in fine rings to fry a golden brown. 5. Add a clove of garlic chopped very fine, a tablespoonful of *crème de riz*, a teaspoonful of turmeric powder, one of powdered cloves and cinnamon, a little salt, a teaspoonful of sugar ; fry together, then add the strained liquor from the prawn shells, the water from the grated cocoanut, cook for a few minutes, then add the prawns and cucumber, and let it remain as it is for $\frac{1}{2}$ hour. 6. Slowly re-heat, adding the milk from the cocoanut. 7. Serve in small brown flat fireproof egg dishes with handles, encircled by plain boiled rice which could alternatively be handed separately.

Veal, so tough and dark in its country birthplace, seems to become milk-white and tender in London, where Jewish butchers or French speciality importers produce it in perfection. " There is many a man for whom the devil lies in wait at the kidney end of a loin of veal," said a famous wit. So this might make a suitable dish to follow, and should be carefully braised, a good stuffing tactfully inserted, or added as a garnish in balls, together with some curls of crisp bacon and midget sausages. A moist purée of sorrel and well-browned potatoes would be suitable for the accompanying vegetables.

A *Salad Course* as habitually given now at

American luncheon parties might furnish a pleasing variety from established usage, and for the central dish a large green bowl containing a mixture of green or sugar corn of the largest shelled variety (as sold in tins by American grocery importers), freshened and flavoured with a little whipped cream, pepper, and red celery salt, and surrounded by pieces of white endive lubricated with oil and vinegar. Or a fruit mixture might be preferred, such as sliced banana, apple shavings, and white grapes, mixed with some cream and set round with green hearts of lettuce or curly endive moistened with salad oil and lemon juice. With this serve very hot crisp biscuits, of the cracker variety or home-made water ones, and a fresh cream cheese; or try transparent slices of gruyère surrounding a heap of freshly-grated roquefort.

In Paris, *Gauffrettes*, or *Waffles*, are always a popular and inexpensive entremet, and the irons with which to make them are readily procurable there. Here waffles are more

A CHRISTMAS LUNCHEON

often seen in the Caledonian Market or in process of manufacture in the purlieus of the Adelphi than at the tables of the well-to-do, but if made according to the recipe below and speeded from fire to dining-table they should meet with the welcome they deserve. Ingredients :—

Two dessertspoonfuls of fine flour, mixed with 1 of white sugar distinctly flavoured with vanilla pod, adding 4 yolks of eggs and ¼ lb. butter creamed with a spoon. Whip the whites of the eggs separately and then whip these together, and incorporate them with the other ingredients. Have ready the heated and greased waffle tongs, and fill one side with the mixture. Close and cook on a bright heat till pale brown, serving on a warmed dish with vanilla flavoured powdered sugar snowed over. Butter the tongs between each waffle, which should take some 2 minutes each to cook. The accompaniment of a pretty glass jug or dainty bowl with cream lightly whipped, or a sauce-boat of hot golden syrup or maple sugar, would be welcome, but not indispensable.

A compote of fruit might, if liked, be provided as an alternative, and since delicious little yellow *Mirabelles* are rarely seen except in town they might be something of a novelty, and most big Stores produce them in tins or bottles.

After a fortifying cup of coffee, the shoppers will return with renewed zest to their afternoon campaign, and when a Christmas thank-offering subsequently arrives—as it may—receive it in the spirit of Theocritus, who wrote : " Surely great grace goes with a little gift, and all the offerings of a friend are precious."

XVIII

COTTAGE HOSPITALITY

THE courage and cheerful fortitude so universally shown by all classes and ages of our countrywomen became one of the platitudes of the closing years of the Great War; and although this spirit is no longer publicly acclaimed and beribboned as in the limelight days of National Service, many who have come down in the world are keeping it alive by gallant and uncomplaining toil, sweeping the rooms and cooking the dinner, mothering the family and cheering the bread-winner, within those narrow homes whither the vicissitudes of fortune have driven the dispossessed in yearly increasing numbers. Such are not the cottages of gentility with double coach-houses, where the pride that apes humility caused the devil to grin when he took his malicious walks abroad. Rather are they the last entrenchments of those whose treasure is no longer on earth, and who, like a certain gallant and high-born youth, have been content to take " Ich dien " for their motto and practice. Many such are daily learning to solve startling problems of house and kitchen, of garden and farm, in wholly unwonted surroundings, and in the thick housemaid's gloves and strong brogues which have replaced the 16-button Peau de Suèdes and the dainty Court shoes of their luxurious past, are practising the making of drudgery divine. The question of future social relations have, however, to be faced, for our friendships cannot always be inspired and limited by purely geographical considerations. Is it best to make the clean cut, definitely breaking with the old life of hall and hunting field, of town, sport, or watering-place, with all their good comradeship and easy hospitalities, or can we keep as far as may be in touch with our real friends, offering such simple and rare entertainment

as changed circumstances permit ? Can we
not, without overstraining modest resources
of storeroom and purse, make adequate
provision for occasional friends from town
who might welcome a health-giving change
to country air from the confinement of the
city ? Or with the lure of lawn-tennis, skat-
ing, or the proximity of golf or river, entice
sometimes those whom we should sorely
miss permanently out of our lives ?

A Frenchwoman recently wrote to her
friend describing the ideal valet de chambre
she required and begging for help in her
quest. Back came the answer : " Ah ! mon
amie, si je trouve ton homme, je l'épouse ! "
So rash and irrevocable a step should surely
prove unnecessary, for the ancient wisdom
holds that there are as good fish in the sea
as ever came out of the water ; and when we
seek diligently for the working housekeeper
or homely person of middle age, Nature,
who is said to abhor a vacuum, may still
be trusted to fill it from her countryside.
Let us, then, remember the words of General

Foch : " Il ne faut rien prendre au tragique, mais tout au sérieux," and consider a few suggestions here offered for mid-day meal or simple supper, all within the compass of any painstaking pair of hands, of any kitchen fire stoked with brains, trusting the keen country air to furnish the required sauce. Let your dinner ware be gay but cheap, your table appointments bright and unexpected rather than costly. A bowl of winter evergreen, a jar of wild flowers for decoration, home-made bread and farmhouse cream and butter, oatcake from the griddle, and buttermilk scones or potato drops with blackberry jelly, and golden honeycomb if your friends stay to tea, will be " in the picture " and richly enjoyable. For drink at dinner or supper a glass jug of cider or lemonade for those aglow with health and exercise, or a toby of hot spiced beer and rummers by the fireside, if the season be wintry, and they will not ask for wine.

Potage Maigre, in a brown marmite for four. Take an egg-sized piece of butter, 2

small onions, 1 white head of celery, 1
cabbage lettuce, some finely - chopped
parsley, 1 water biscuit, 1 quart milk, 1
egg yolk. Melt the butter in the stewpan, dice the onions and celery into it,
shred the lettuce, add the parsley finely
chopped. Cook and shake over the
fire for some 15 minutes with lid on,
but don't let it brown. Stir in the
water biscuit, finely crushed ; add the
quart of milk *boiling*, and let all boil on
gently for 45 minutes. Withdraw, adding pepper and salt to taste. Pour this
on to the yolk of an egg mixed with a
little cream in a basin ; stir together,
re-heat, and serve in a warmed marmite
soup pot very hot. If too thick stir in
a little hot milk.

Chicken Pilaf.

Put into a stewpan ¼ lb. butter, 2 medium-
sized onions cut into dice, and fry with
lid on to a pale brown. Add ½ lb. rice,
a pinch of saffron tied in muslin (for
removal when rice is cooked), and 2
breakfast-cupfuls of stock ; cook 30 minutes, add 2 oz. stoned raisins ; cook another 30 minutes, stir gently together,
adding pepper and salt. Braise a
chicken or pheasant, or even a rabbit,

carve into joints, and lay at one end of a long dish—the rice heaped at the other with some tiny well-fried onion rings, and some almonds split and browned added to the rice.

Scotch Collops.

Remove all fat from 1½ lb. rump steak, or fresh mutton fillet, pass through a mincing machine, melt a small egg-sized piece of butter in a frying pan, add a tablespoonful of finely-chopped onion, fry a golden brown, then add the minced meat, stirring with a spoon to keep the mince separate. Sprinkle over a little chopped parsley, salt, and pepper, place in a hot fireproof dish, garnish with sippets of fried bread or toast, and serve as soon as cooked. It only takes about 5 minutes to cook the collops, which make excellent food for children or convalescents.

Choux à la Fermière.

Use no soda in boiling your freshly gathered cabbage, and when half done, cut the leaves apart, shred them, and simmer gently for some 10 minutes in one to two cupfuls of milk to which has been added a heaped tablespoonful of flour dissolved in half a cup of water and worked to a smooth paste, adding one tablespoonful of butter and one of margarine, and a good pinch of salt. Two or three tablespoonfuls of cream would improve this sauce, and coarsely ground black pepper is the best flavouring, added at the last. This improved form of cabbage is welcomed by many who have hitherto looked with hostility on its homely virtue.

Bread and Butter Pudding, for six persons.

Cut about six thin slices of bread and butter from a tin loaf, remove crust, cut into squares or rounds. Arrange in a nice white buttered dish or oven-proof glass oval. Add a few stoned raisins or well-soaked sultanas, sprinkle with castor sugar. Break 2 whole eggs and one extra yolk into a basin, whisk up, pour on $\frac{1}{2}$ pint of hot milk flavoured with vanilla, and pour this on to bread and butter ; then embellish the top with some halved glacé cherries and acorn-sized pieces of crushed loaf sugar. Cook to attractive brownness in a slow oven for $\frac{3}{4}$ hour, and serve with fresh cream. Good both hot or cold.

As an alternative for summer, an old-
fashioned china bowl of *Junket and Cream*
is hard to beat, but its possibilities of
tasteless watery insipidity are as great
and more familiar than its qualities of delicious simplicity and creamy velvet wholesomeness.

Take 1 quart of freshest milk, and warm
it in a stewpan to blood-heat, some
98 degrees, but not more. Sweeten
it with about 2 tablespoonfuls of castor
sugar, flavoured with a tablespoonful of
rum—or, if preferred, some 6 or 8 drops
of vanilla essence—and into this warmed
and flavoured milk pour 1 tablespoonful
of rennet. Pour all this into the china
or glass bowl in which it will be served
and leave to cool—say from 11 a.m. till
luncheon, or from 4 o'clock till supper-
time—in a cool, shady place. Just before
serving pour over the contents of the
bowl a thin covering of fresh thick
cream. The old fashion of flavouring
a sour watery compound with sprinkled
nutmeg can be honoured in the breach
but not in the observance ; good brown
sugar is a welcome addition handed
round.

COTTAGE HOSPITALITY

N.B.—If parsley should run scarce in the cottage garden, as it often does in summer drought and protracted winter, try green celery tops pulled into small pieces and fried crisp, to eat with your filleted fish or rissoles. It is a most agreeable and surprising substitute.

XIX

CHRISTMAS CHEER

THE great winter feast of the Christian faith,
falling as it does at the same season as that
more ancient festival of the Birthday of the
Sun, reminds us that from the time of the
winter solstice onwards, a new light shines
and a fresh hope has dawned on a dark
world. St. Augustine was wont to exhort
his Christian brethren not to celebrate the
holy day as did the heathen, on account of
the Sun, but on account of Him who made
the Sun, and a curious intermingling of
customs and rites have survived in our
Christian observance of Christmas which
dimly recall ancient and half-forgotten beliefs.
The magical control of the Sun was vested
in certain wizards, who used incantations
around their sacred fires, where the rising of

the Sun and its increasing power was sym-
bolized in the up-springing of the ritual
flames. We still set our plum pudding and
our mince pies on fire, explaining the custom
by considerations of easier digestion and
increased wholesomeness through the burning away of superfluous grease ; but really
we are, as it were, invoking and placating
a mysterious and dimly apprehended power,
who may thus be induced to wax brighter
and warmer, to consume the clouds and the
darkness, and to shine beneficently upon us.

Mistletoe, again, could tell many a tale of
fear and imagination, being itself a visible
emanation of the celestial fire, and unable
to flourish on common soil. Aloft between
earth and sky it still grows and blossoms,
although no longer guarded in sacred groves
by priests and druids. Ornithologists will
explain the precise species and habits of
those birds who devour the seeds and carry
them to these strange propagating grounds
in the high forks of trees—" Il y en a pour
tous les goûts ! "

141

Again, when we decorate our churches and homes with winter greenery, we are carrying on the custom commended by the prophet Isaiah : " The glory of Lebanon shall come unto thee, the fir tree, the pine tree, and the box together, to beautify the place of my sanctuary." For the ancients held that the vital power of trees and green branches could pass into the garments or the armour hung about them, thereby adding life and strength to the wearers ; and in this belief, wreaths and boughs would be brought at special festivals to the altar and hung around the shrine.

Let us, then, keep Christmas with all the time-honoured usages of high festival, and again welcome the *turkey*, with abundant accompaniments of bread sauce and gravy. Let an additional brown fireproof or white metal dish follow it with ample supplies of chestnut darkly braised with good stock, or creamed to a delicious purée with milk and butter. Then will there be room also for midget sausages and tiny crisp curls of bacon, for browned or new potatoes (bottled by the prudent), for grilled mushrooms and little balls of stuffing or precious truffles. These can never all be swiftly or adequately distributed from the one dish. Cranberry sauce can give a suitable variety to the re-appearance of the bird cold next day, and here is a good recipe for a *Réchauffé* after the stages of pulled, grilled, and devilled have been passed, or the varieties of *Cuisses en papilottes*, *Vol-au-vent*, or *Emincé* inside souffléd baked potatoes have been enjoyed.

Butter a stewpan, add rice and a little stock, put in the oven and cook gently with the lid on till a golden colour. Put into a charlotte mould with centre space filled in with turkey or chicken, or game remains, pulled into pieces and warmed in a nice béchamel, adding mushrooms if possible. Cover in the mould with rice, and keep in oven till dishing up. The rice should be rather dry, brittle, and brown outside, retaining a soft and creamy mixture within.

Some people like Christmas pudding to emerge dark and rich from an imprisonment of many weeks in the basin. Those who prefer the light-brown, freshly-made, and more wholesome compound might try this mixture (sufficient for about ten people), known as the

Enchantress Plum Pudding.

Half a pound *each* of bread-crumbs, sultanas, currants, raisins, mixed peel, suet, brown sugar, 4 eggs, and the zest of 2 lemons. Mix and cook in usual way, serving with brandy or orange butter.

A polite Frenchman, after his first experience of English Christmas fare, said with enthusiasm : " Ce que j'adore dans la cuisine anglaise ce sont vos petits mince-pi." The American version of a large open puff-paste tart encircling a deep pond of mince-meat is an agreeable variant, and can equally have its libation of burning brandy. Some crabbed natures like to express their abhorrence of both these sweets : let them substitute a seasonable

Macédoine of Dried Fruits and Cake.

Cut into small pieces some glacé cherries, French plums, raisins, citron peel, dates, and a few crystallized or glacé French apricots, greengages, or pears. Put these into a stewpan with a tinned pine-apple cut into small pieces, with the juice added to the other fruit. Let all get very hot, and place on slices of sponge cake cut in rounds fried in butter to a pale brown on both sides. A dash of rum or maraschino flavouring the mixed fruits can be added — the fruit could be piled into a pyramid on a large round of fried cake divided into sections for convenient helpings.

Should that dark plum-cake covered with almond paste and thick icing, whereby the cook expresses devotion to her family or to her art, be considered too much of a good thing, substitute this *Children's Cake*, made thus :—

Half a pound of butter beaten to a cream with ½ lb. castor sugar ; break in 4 fresh eggs, beating each separately; add gradu-ally ½ lb. flour, then 1 oz. of skinned and chopped pistachio nuts, 1 oz. chopped sweet almonds, ½ lb. glacé cherries halved, the grated rind of a lemon. Mix well ; bake in a moderate oven for some 2 hours. Cover with soft icing, and decorate with more pistachio.

Fortunately, Christmas comes but once a year, even as the poet, in reflective mood, puts it :

> " Therefore are feasts so solemn and so rare,
> Since seldom coming, in the long year set
> Like stones of worth, they thinly placed are,
> Or captain jewels in the Carcanet."

Let it, then, be kept by joyful hearts and with rejoicing, and while we have time let us do good to all men.

XX

TRAY FOOD

ILL-HEALTH may be said to resemble greatness
in that some are born to it, some achieve it,
and some have it thrust upon them. The
number of those who, for one cause or another
must perforce dwell apart, eating the bread
of exile, is no inconsiderable one, and in
the interests of the invalids—temporary or
permanent—of the disabled, of the baby's
mother, of the rest-cure cases, of those in
quarantine after or before infectious disease,
of those recovering from surgical operations,
it may be useful to consider how meals, of
vital importance to their comfort and resto-
ration to health, may be made more acceptable than they often are. Most of us have
suffered during temporary disablement from
exasperating trays, all the most important

items—salt, pepper, mustard, sugar, bread, milk—omitted, their glass and crockery appointments so ragged and ill-assorted that no nourishment could appear attractive in their company, and the food itself chosen and presented without one touch of the capacity for taking pains which we are told is of the family of genius, and which can outweigh mere culinary skill or lavish expenditure on delicacies.

More attention to the technique of tray meals, then, is undoubtedly called for, and every house should possess attractive trays in various sizes and japanned in cheerful colours, leaf green, lemon yellow, sunset red, sea blue. Though light in weight they must be capacious, having " a parapidge for safety " and being easily allied to the necessary bed table. Also, they should have allotted tray-cloths and napkins in gay and harmonizing effects, their china, glass, and other accessories daintily matched or contrasted. The hot-water plate and cover, companion of those long-drawn-out meals of our nursery days, can be retrieved and furbished up ; lustre ware both of silver and gold give a touch of brightness to the tea or breakfast sets; fireproof jugs and dishes of green, brown, or blue, and oven glass in small pie-dish shapes, or round with *cloche* covers for eggs and fish *au gratin*, or mushrooms, vegetables, or cooked fruit, will ensure heat, which is a primary necessity. Of late, jugs constructed on thermos principles, and commonly used in America for iced water, are on sale in our first-rate china and glass shops, and these adequately preserve the extremes of heat and cold for an unpunctual sick-room, surely a great consideration where sleep often counts more than nourishment. Small food-warming trays, with jugs and toast racks, over a tiny spirit lamp will easily keep toast and coffee hot should its arrival be untimely or its consumption delayed.

Remember that the whole tone of the day can be set into a happy major key instead of into a mournful minor one by the mere aspect of the breakfast tray. A cheerful

149

cherry—glacé or fresh—will render irresistible the skilfully-prepared and iced grape fruit on a hot day; a seedless orange halved and treated in the same way, beautified by green leaves of its own, or the nearest resembling foliage (and even villa gardens can boast a laurustinus bush); a gay pottery saucer of thin slices of banana with brown sugar and cream, a slice of melon, a tiny bunch of grapes, summer fruits in their seasons, and the health-giving apple accompanied by its ingenious little plated corer and wooden platter—all these may render nourishment welcome. A bunch of violets or primroses, a single rose, a sprig of heather, a spray of lemon verbena would bring a reminder of fresh life and loveliness from the outdoor world. To those bored with tea, coffee, and cocoa, even at their best, the unexpected and clean wholesomeness of well-made *Cocoa Nibs* might be welcome.

Take 2 quarts cold water to a teacupful of unbruised cocoa nibs, and let simmer without boiling in an open saucepan till reduced by half. Add 1 pint cold water and boil till reduced to half the quantity; add a second pint, and again reduce by boiling; finally add a third pint of cold water, and simmer till reduced to half. Never put on the lid during the process, which will take from 5 to 6 hours. If properly made it is a beautiful claret colour and free from all bitterness, and should be served with hot milk, cream, and a little coffee sugar.

For the mid-day meal serve as the principal " plat " a nicely cut and fried bread *canapé* some six inches by four inches and one inch thick, and on to this spread a thick layer of well-made purée of chestnut with a couple of stoned and heated black plums at each corner. On this lay several delicately-cut slices of pheasant or turkey roasted or braised, and a little good gravy poured very hot over it. Or if chicken be the order of the day, make a bed of savoury rice on your *canapé*, enriching it with sultanas steeped in hot white wine or stock, and mixed with almonds split and grilled brown, and pieces of the breast laid on it. Again, slices of goose or duck reposing on a mattress of thick apple sauce above the *canapé*, or partridge breasts resting on softly-mashed potatoes and some mushrooms buttered, grilled, and added piping hot. Even the familiar slice of roast mutton from the family joint would acquire additional merit if supplemented by a creamy layer of mashed turnips, and a nice little pile of capers or a soubise sauce to add zest. All these might appear as off-shoots from the family dinner.

To vary the pudding course, make this *Cutchi*, or savoury custard, good hot or cold, in small round oven glass or white china individual ramekin cases, and send with it gossamer slices of brown bread toasted brittle in a slow oven.

Milk $\frac{1}{2}$ pint, 3 whole eggs, 2 oz. freshly grated parmesan cheese, a little mixed mustard, nepaul pepper, and salt to taste. Beat well, and steam $\frac{1}{2}$ hour, the water boiling when you put the little cases into the stewpan, but not after.

TRAY FOOD

Tea-time, the invalid's happiest moment, might produce these little *Quaker Oat Pyramids* which can boast the four modern cardinal virtues of novelty, niceness, wholesomeness, and economy :—

Quaker Oats ½ lb., butter 6 oz., castor sugar 5 oz., 8 drops essence of almonds. Oil the butter, mix the oats and sugar together. Form a well, into which pour the butter and essence. Mix lightly into heaped tablespoonfuls on a specially well-greased baking sheet, and put into a very slow oven for about ¾ hour. Do not remove from baking sheet till cold, else they crumble. The cakes should rise in little pyramids some 3 inches high from a base round as a claret glass rim. Half this quantity will make ten cakes, but as they don't keep well, let nurse or nursery enjoy the surplus.

XXI

DANCE AND SUPPER

THE New Year has always begun socially
with festivities, but surely the practice of
dancing has never been so universal and con-
tinuous as in the present time. The homes of
England, as well as the provincial town halls
and newer village institutes, have of late years
followed the example of the London restaurants and dance clubs, echoing nightly,
and often from tea-time onwards, to the
strains of orchestra or jazz band, of pianola
or gramophone. Even the churches are
showing their widened sympathies by the
promotion of dancing and cards within their
folds. The admonitions of two widely dis-
severed counsellors of youth would in these
days have been wholly superfluous. " Sacrifice to the graces ! " reiterated Plato to his

disciples : " Delay not to take the best dancing-master you can hear of," wrote Lord Chesterfield to his son. And could they but revisit the glimpses of the moon, would not they too be enslaved by the prevailing passion, which, dominating old and young alike, has transformed the thoughts and habits of busy and serious persons to a surprising extent. The chaperon also is forging her way slowly back to an almost obsolete bench, whence she, too, can join the dance. Eating and drinking—as always where people congregate in numbers—have become a matter of acute interest and urgent effort. " The oldest and youngest are at work with the strongest," wrote the observant Wordsworth ; " there are forty feeding like one ! " Where space is a consideration, it may be well to organize refreshments continuously throughout the evening, thus avoiding the special crush inseparable from a definite supper hour with its disappointments and delay ; and the musicians, adequately fortified early and late, would only then require brief interludes for refreshment and no prolonged supper interval. Round tables seating eight to twelve, supplemented by quite small ones tucked in where possible, are always more popular than a stand-up buffet; and if tea, coffee, lemonade, and ices can be dispensed from a separate tea-room, it lightens the strain on the supper-tables. Here is a recipe for some nice biscuits and for orangeade, the speciality of a famous Parisian restaurateur, for the tea-room.

Cinnamon Biscuits.

Three oz. butter, 3 oz. castor sugar, 6 oz. flour, 1 egg, 1 teaspoonful powdered cinnamon. Beat butter and sugar to a cream. Mix cinnamon with flour, adding it gradually; moisten this mixture with beaten egg till a stiff paste. Roll out, and cut into cakes with a round cutter; sprinkle with chopped almonds. Put on a baking sheet in a moderate oven.

Orangeade.

For every 3 quart glass cup-jug, take the rinds of 2 lemons and 2 oranges, peeled very thin ; place these in *bain-marie* with 1 dessertspoonful of white sugar to each orange, and bring to boiling-point. Cut 6 oranges and 2 lemons in halves, squeeze and strain their juices into a thick white kitchen jug ; add the syrup made from the rinds, etc., and put on ice. Just before serving in glass cup-jug, add an iced syphon of soda, or 3 small bottles of soda, or soda added to plain water, as preferred. Use blood oranges when procurable, otherwise colour with a drop or two of cochineal and float 2 or 3 slices of the fresh fruit. Always serve very cold.

On the supper-room tables may be assembled all the most attractive things that can be devised for easy consumption (preferably with fork and spoon) under the alert supervision of one detailed to refresh and replace food and drink before the changing guests. Soup of the clear consommé type should be available early and late, and there is generally a special run on it when the party breaks up : twenty quarts for a hundred guests and twenty-four quarts of lemonade

or orangeade would be an approximate provision. A large but delicately made *Quenelle* of cream of chicken or veal, moulded
the size of a dessert spoon, with a few peas or
vegetables reduced almost to a glaze, placed
in the centre of the quenelle, and covered
in with a little more of the chicken cream,
and poached lightly in water, kept hot, and
one slipped into each portion of the consommé
when served, gives distinction to the soup.
Or *Clear Tomato Soup* with a spot of whipped
cream on a tiny croustade, or *Consommé à
la Indienne*, made with chicken carcasses and
lightly flavoured with grated cocoanut, curry
paste, and a few grains of rice, would be a
little out of the common run.

Sandwiches can show infinite variety,
and the popular kinds are too well known
to require description, but here are two
sorts, perhaps rather less obvious :—

Œufs à la Crême.
Cut round slices, wine-glass size, from
French roll or bread, boil the eggs hard,
pass through a sieve, season with pepper

158

and salt. Then whip some cream and stir in the eggs lightly, spread thickly on the buttered bread, add a soupçon of chopped lettuce or cress, and lay the twin buttered slice very lightly over it.

The same rounds *à la Guyon*, spread with shrimp or salmon paste, a slice of peeled tomato cut the long way of the fruit, and made into an oblong sandwich with a sprinkle of chopped cress, are good.

For a good cold *Cream of Chicken* for the supper table, steam a large plump fowl till tender. When cold pound the meat, and pass through a hair sieve mixed with enough cream to make it light, season to taste, add 3 or 4 leaves of gelatine dissolved. When nearly set, pour it into a plain round charlotte or brick-shaped mould previously lined with aspic of the chicken stock, turn out, and serve very cold with a garnish of shredded and creamed celery, or a fruit salad, or chopped aspic and cress. A similar treatment of lobster makes a good *mousse*, and the economist can use whiting for its basis. Both these can also be served in small individual mould shapes, if preferred, round a centre of salad.

Large *Silver Bowls of Macédoine,* made with Bartlett pears quartered, Cape plums halved, peeled, and stoned, and some fresh pine-apple with plenty of claret-coloured syrup is a safe stand-by. As also are glass bowls of *Tangerine Jelly*, each made with 12 tangerines, 1 quart water, 1 oz. gelatine, and from 6 to 8 oz. sugar, treated as for lemon jelly, with sections of skinned and pipped tangerine showing through the jelly, and a little sprinkling of finely-shredded skin ; a small glass of curaçoa or yellow chartreuse improves it.

A boiled turkey, robed in white béchamel, spotted with black truffle peelings and attended by a sugar-cured ham, can shelter on the serving table till required. Its presence gives confidence to the anxious hostess, and wholesome food to the wise and prudent. When champagne is absent, this cider cup, as served at a restaurant of world-wide reputation, may possibly be preferred to wine :—

For a 3 quart glass jug of *Cider Cup*, place 2 quart bottles of cider and 2 bottles of soda-water, or a syphon, on ice for 2 or 3 hours according to season.

Just before serving, put in a jug 2 oz. castor sugar, a liqueur glass of brandy, a wine glass of sherry, $\frac{1}{2}$ wine glass curaçoa, and a wine glass of *sirop de grenadine*. Pour in the cider and soda water, float pieces of whatever fruit you may have— apples, oranges, pine-apple, strawberries, peach, cherries—with a slice or two of cucumber, and a lump of ice. A liberal dash of orange juice is a great improvement.

XXII

FOOD FOR ARTISTS AND SPEAKERS

MUSICAL and dramatic artists as well as
public speakers and lecturers find that they
cannot give out their best very soon after
a substantial meal. When their effort is
over, they are often either nervously exhausted and disinclined to eat—in which
case they require nourishing but easily-
digested and tempting food; or else they are
so hungry that they eat freely of anything
available, with resultant indigestion and
restlessness, just when they most urgently
require calm and refreshing sleep before
another public appearance. Those who have
sown unto us spiritual things have a claim
on the harvest of our worldly things; for,
unless well cared for materially, they can
neither raise mortals to the skies, nor yet

call angels down. Parliamentary elections, too, have horrid possibilities of recurrence, with their nightmare train of exhausting effort and disordered home-life; and a little care in the selection and preparation of suitable foods may even turn the tide of fortune, and enable politicians to scorn fatigue or illness and lead on to victory.

A slight supplement to a late 5 o'clock tea is the usual practice for those with a public appearance before them, and eggs, boiled, poached, or *en cocotte*, with savoury sandwiches are the most obvious addition to the tea-table. A small white china ramekin case filled with this quickly-made *Mousse of Egg and Sardine*, to be spread on thin crisp toast, is often useful, and within the compass of the humblest cook. Take a hard-boiled egg and pass it through a sieve into a basin; skin and bone four small sardines and pass through a sieve. Mix these two with a filbert-sized piece of fresh butter; add pepper, and moisten all with a little cream if available. Good also for breakfast as a change from marmalade.

Mrs. Gladstone's practice of sending her husband into battle on an egg-flip, cleverly produced at the psychological moment, can be imitated with this *Frothed Wine Soup*, good for a prima donna or pianist soon going into action, and can be made by anybody who can whisk an egg.

> Beat 3 yolks of quite fresh eggs to a froth with a whisk over the fire, adding a small teaspoonful each of fine flour and white sugar, half a bottle of white wine, and half that quantity of water. Whisk till it comes to the boil, then take it off and serve immediately before the froth subsides. This quantity amply suffices for two.

At a Paris restaurant much frequented by the stars of the Comédie Française, these *Œufs Pochés en Surprise* were recently *the* popular " plat," of which the chef obligingly communicated the recipe to an artist patron.

> Carefully poach as many new-laid eggs as required. When done, slip them into

a basin of cold water ; allow 2 thin slices from a good ham for each egg. Place the drained and trimmed egg on a slice of ham, putting another slice on top, repeating this for each egg. Lay them delicately in a long dish, sufficiently deep for their covering over in some aspic jelly, not very stiff, and delicately flavoured with tarragon. When set, cut them out with an oval tin cutter, and with a fish-slice place them on a silver dish, garnish with green salad, and serve with bread and butter sandwiches. They appear like midget galantines of savoury jelly, concealing the softly cooked egg hidden inside, and are both light and nourishing.

For those requiring more solid food, and yet unable to face suppers such as mixed grills, or sausages and mashed potatoes with lager beer, here are two recipes which might also be useful for other occasions.

Soles au Gratin.

Butter a long fireproof dish ; fillet some fair-sized soles ; chop 2 large mushrooms, a piece of fat bacon the size of a walnut, a sprig of thyme and parsley,

and a shalot very fine; mix with 2 handfuls of fine bread-crumbs, pepper and
salt, and the juice of ½ lemon. Spread
a layer of the mixture at the bottom of
the dish, on it place the fillets of soles,
cover with the remainder, place in a
moderate oven for about 30 minutes,
and just before serving pour a glass of
white wine over, and serve in the same
dish.

Poulet à la Crême.

Cut 1 or 2 small tender chickens in half,
rub them with salt and papprika pepper.
Put a good lump of butter in small
pieces into a stewpan with some thin
slices of streaky bacon. Cover these
with a layer of onions cut into thin
rings and put the pan on the fire. When
the contents begin to smoke, add the
half chickens, and let them stew on a
slow fire for 1½ hour, when they should
be a light brown. Remove from pan,
carve into pieces and lay on a hot dish.
Replace stewpan on fire, and add ½ pint
sour cream, stirring constantly with a
wooden spoon. Pour this sauce upon
the chickens, and serve very hot; on
no account add water or stock to this
sauce.

FOOD FOR ARTISTS AND SPEAKERS

Tartines Tricolor made a popular supper delicacy at a house beloved by musicians and actors in pre-war days.

> Take thin round slices 2½ to 3 inches across from a long French roll or fresh loaf, butter sparingly, and lay slantingly across these open rounds thin strips alternately of white chicken (or turkey), of red tongue (or ham), of pickled cucumber (or mildly salted gherkin), varied by a thin fillet of anchovy washed in milk if too salt, and dish these flat with a light sprinkling of small cress in the centre.

An alternative might be the small oblong crisp toast sandwiches popular at West End bridge clubs, with a tiny roll, little finger size, of crisply fried streaky bacon, served in covered muffin dishes piping hot, and welcome on a chilly night.

On hot evenings the spent artist might dream, like the Sick King in Bokhara, "of cherries served in drifts of snow," but muscat grapes, skinned and pipped, reposing in a pond of delicious calvesfoot lemon jelly in a flat glass dish, would be more wholesome and nourishing. Or when muscats are out of season, try this reviving

Gelée à la Bourgogne.

Half a bottle of fairly good claret, 3 oz. white sugar, half a sherry glass of brandy, the thin rind and juice of one good lemon, ½ teacup raspberry jam or jelly, boiled together with 4 or 5 leaves of gelatine according to temperature, or ½ oz. of isinglass. Strain through a muslin, and set in a mould with a hollow centre for the reception of sweetened whipped cream. In hot weather use ice for stiffening jelly and cream.

These should all prove good preludes to " Great Nature's second course, chief nourisher in life's great feast."

XXIII

BACHELORS ENTERTAINING

LET us picture a bachelor living in a modest London house or in country surroundings near to his work, with a married couple, or oftener a working housekeeper, to look after him. Being constantly entertained by his friends and relations, he naturally desires occasionally to offer something in return: Problems of hospitality for such are oftenest solved by inviting their friends to a restaurant dinner or play—an agreeable but expensive solution—or by invitation cards for luncheons or teas at some race meeting or popular cricket match, when all responsibility is taken over by the club or contractor. This sort of entertaining, however, welcome as it may often be, seems to lack the personal note, for we do not really know our friends until

169

we can visualize them in their own surroundings, and take interest in the gathered treasures or the pursuits of their homes. A host, moreover, feels and appears at a greater advantage by his own fireside than in the garish setting of a public restaurant, and might well say with Touchstone : " When I was at home, I was in a better place ! " Time often handicaps the host who has succumbed to the temptation of admitting the disturbing presence of woman into his sacred seclusion, for he may find it irksome to consider dinner problems whilst bacon and eggs are yet in his mouth, and the morning train relentlessly approaches. Possibly, then, a few suggestions of simple but not too obvious dishes may not come amiss, and should be more generally useful than a single detailed menu, for purses and tastes, seasons and cooking facilities, differ widely. Moreover, any of these dishes can be exchanged or supplemented for popular and easily obtainable things such as bottled turtle, or tinned tomato soups, with caviare and foie

gras or more homely *hors d'œuvres* to precede
them. If the fish market be near, oysters,
lobster, or dressed crab might be summoned,
or the help of the cooked provision merchant
invoked for dressed meats and pies, for ham,
tongue, or galantine, and the recently de-
veloped pastry-cook artist might delight and
surprise with his wonderful creations in
cream tarts and decorated cakes. But there
is surely a want of individuality about enter-
tainments built exclusively on preserved and
ready dressed provisions, and the dictum of
an eminent Victorian housekeeper still holds :
" Give your friends what you have your-
selves ; only have enough of it, and make it
a little nicer."

Stychy Polonaise is an easy and comforting
soup, the speciality of a gay little half-
underground restaurant in distant Warsaw.

> Cut in square-shaped pieces some car-
> rots, turnips, leeks, celery, cabbage, ac-
> cording to quantity required. Fry these
> in butter with a pinch of salt and sugar,
> add some good brown stock sufficient
> for expected guests, and let all simmer

gently for about an hour ; remove any grease. Thicken with a dessertspoonful of brown flour liquefied with stock, boil up, and add a little cream before serving.

Cod and Oysters au Gratin, sufficient for four persons, would be a good selection for winter.

Steam about 1½ lb. of middle of cod ; when nearly cooked remove skin and bone, break into pieces, make a good creamy white sauce, put the fish into a greased fireproof dish with six or more oysters bearded and cut in half and pour over the sauce. Next sprinkle over liberally some browned buttered bread-crumbs, a little freshly-grated cheese, a restrained dusting of mild red pepper, and a squeeze of lemon juice. Place the dish in the oven to get very hot. A few pieces of boiled cod's liver dotted here and there may be added with advantage. This makes an excellent winter luncheon dish, and with a little practice a plain cook can accomplish it to perfection.

Boiled Mutton is a dish reminiscent of the seaside boarding-house table, but no less a connoisseur than King Edward VII. was especially fond of this transfiguring version of it.

Boil the best end of a neck of tender mutton (four to six cutlets), dip in oiled butter, roll in coarse white dried breadcrumbs, and grill for some 15 minutes. Serve in a large oven-proof dish surrounded by small piles of nicely-prepared vegetables, such as new potatoes finished in butter and chopped parsley, with some small glazed onions, and sprouts, carrots, beans, turnips, peas or chopped sprue braised in a little stock and butter, all nicely cut and disposed around. Send with it a clear gravy in a sauce-bowl with plenty of capers and finely-chopped pickled gherkin, and in addition sprinkle both of these last items sparingly over the grilled meat.

Savoury Puddings can be made with a chicken jointed and cut up, some ½ lb. sausages cut into biggish pieces, and some veal collops ; or alternatively with game such as plovers or black game, grouse or partridge, past their first youth. They require the addition of thin slices of tender steak rolled up small or enwrapping the boned joints of game varied by slices of cooked ham, and perhaps a kidney or two cut up with small mushrooms is an improvement. Good gravy made from the livers and carcass bones of the birds, with seasoning of herbs, chopped parsley, salt, and pepper are necessary, but given good material no sauce or wine should be required. Interline a buttered pudding basin with a light suet paste, chop a little meat small for furnishing the ground floor, so to speak, add the other ingredients, and cover over with paste. Boil very slowly, for some 2 hours or more, serving in the same basin neatly dressed up in a clean napkin.

Caramel of Oranges and Cream is a nice and recently evolved sweet.

Make a salad of thick slices of orange, carefully excluding pips, pith, and skin, and lay in a glass dish or pretty bowl. Make a thin syrup with the escaped juice and white sugar, adding a little extra juice if required, and pour on this. Take ¼ lb. loaf sugar, and stir in enamelled or copper pan with ½ tumbler of water over the fire till melted, and then let it boil into a not too dark caramel, taking some 10 minutes. Pour this out to get cold and stiffen ; crush it coarsely when hard and crisp, and shake it over the fruit. Cover all with some well-whipped cream—$\frac{1}{4}$ pint will suffice—and on to this sprinkle a few almonds, browned and roughly chopped.

For a savoury, make or buy some small round very thin water biscuits. Spread these when cold with a mixture made of a table-spoonful of fresh butter, a dash of Worcester sauce, and a teaspoonful of either chutney or a thick hot sauce such as *Diable*, all worked into a thin paste. Put the biscuits into a quick oven for some five minutes. Serve very hot, with a very cold fresh cream cheese, and some curls of celery or radishes.

There are pauses of service in the best regulated dining-rooms, when solace is sought in crumbling or nibbling something. Salted almonds are expensive, and by many thought indigestible ; they can be understudied by a packet of the American cereal *Puffed Wheat*. A few spoonfuls of this, crisped hot in the oven and lying invitingly on small mother-o'-pearl shells, or in some such decorative and labour-saving receptacles before each guest, will comfort the shy, stem the torrent of the fluent-obvious, and generally promote a flow of that pleasant conversation, such as the late Lord Acton yearned for when he bade his friend remember that "One touch of *ill* nature makes the whole world kin."

XXIV

FOOD FOR TRAVELLERS

THE birds have not a monopoly of migration in our restless age. Every year winter sports, Riviera sunshine, Italian culture, or the lure of Monte Carlo summon the athletic, the invalid, the student, or the mere pleasure-seeker, in ever increasing numbers to pursue the insubstantial form of happiness to their chosen resorts.

Travellers in these times are reverting to the old-fashioned habit of taking their journey food with them, some actuated by motives of economy if the party be numerous, others by the discomforts of that dark and perilous pilgrimage from remote parts of a swaying train to the crowded restaurant car. Some have a preference for the food of their own choice, others would limit the opportunity

of the hostile microbe. For prolonged jour-
neys, then, with all their attendant uncer-
tainties, it may be worth while to pack the
fitted luncheon basket, and on it to super-
impose a flat strapped overflow receptacle
containing adequate provision of food and
drink, if the way be long and the night cold.
Most cooks lack both the imagination and
experience necessary for such journey requirements, and have thereby brought the
home-packed hamper into disrepute; but
there is no reason why ham sandwiches and
desiccated seed-cake should be the sole and
inevitable refreshments provided.

Attractive presentation of travellers' fare
has a large share in its success. Many of
the big Stores, particularly those with American connections, specialize in the provision
of papier-maché plates, dishes, and jars, of
collapsible cups, and paper napkins. The
food should be daintily packed in grease-
proof paper with an outer wrapping of fools-
cap tied with fine twine and the contents
marked outside. A nest of horn or alumi-

nium drinking cups, together with a wash-
able roll of American cloth or silver aeroplane
waterproof to hold cheap knives, forks, and
spoons, can easily be provided if the basket
be not a fully fitted one. For the food itself
here are some suggestions, which must be
dependent on individual tastes, on the length
of the journey, on the purse of the traveller.
Hard-boiled eggs accompanied by green
sandwiches of lettuce or watercress, a small
wisp of oriental salt, or Cerebos, mixed
with coarsely-ground black pepper for each
traveller, are always a good stand-by ; the
breasts of chickens or pheasants, partridges
or grouse, enriched perhaps with a little
purée of foie gras or thin coating of savoury
aspic ; a salad of cold potato and lettuce,
sparingly moistened with thin mayonnaise in
a grease-paper-lined cardboard dish, can be
the *pièce de résistance*. Packets of sandwiches can be multiplied according to numbers and need, and varied indefinitely, for,
good as those of nicely-made ham, tongue,
or pressed beef can be, they have that fam-

iliarity which often breeds indifference, and it is wonderful what can be done to invest them with surprised interest by a touch of chutney, or Cumberland sauce, of tarragon flavoured vinegar on their green salad addition, of a slice of beetroot powdered with chopped gherkin, or of tomato sprinkled with capers. Sandwiches of foie gras of well-known brands are for the rich, but this humbler counterfeit can be recommended.

Home-made Foie Gras.

One pound of chicken livers or 2 goose livers, about ¼ lb. fat bacon. Cut the bacon into small pieces, put into a frying-pan and fry it slowly, then add the livers cut up small, and sprig of thyme and bay leaf. Add a tablespoonful of brandy or sherry and fry altogether about 10 minutes, then put into the mortar and pound well, removing herbs ; pass through a fine wire sieve, then mix up with a little cream, salt, and pepper. Put into a pot, pressing all well together, and pour over a little clarified butter to keep out the air. Small pieces of truffle are a great addition to the flavour, and should be added with the cream.

FOOD FOR TRAVELLERS

Sandwiches of thinnest gruyère between biscuits, or bread spread with green butter are excellent, and this is easily made and welcome in winter and summer, giving variety to the cheese course.

Savoury Green Butter.

A ¼ lb. good fresh butter. A couple of handfuls of spinach, boiled, drained, and passed through a hair sieve, the pulp obtained saved in a bowl. Bone and wipe off the oil of 6 anchovies, pass through sieve and save pulp. Mince finely a tablespoonful of curled parsley, ditto a teaspoonful of capers. Colour the butter first by working in the spinach greening, then add the other ingredients and turn into a block or an attractive small mould, or use for sandwiches after hardening in the ice box. The inventive cook will vary her butter by using sardines, lobster, prawns, crab meat, and flavouring with cress, gherkins, olives, etc., and colouring red with lobster coral, or mixing with crab.

Sandwiches of fruit for the children are popular. Round slices of banana sprinkled with orange juice and white centrifugal sugar, or of thinly-cut apple with grated walnuts, sandwiches of cream cheese with a thin spread of red currant jelly, of egg with sardine or anchovy, of celery shredded and creamed and sprinkled with plentiful yolk of hard-boiled egg, sandwiches of sponge-cake spread with chocolate or coffee icing, sandwiches of pastry with jam or glazed with thin caramel. Here is a recipe for lemon cheese cake mixture to fill light puff paste tartlets, for though a familiar dish it admits of as many classes as the Tripos, and this should be in Class I.

Lemon Cheese Cake Mixture.

Two large lemons, 3 oz. butter, $\frac{1}{2}$ lb. lump sugar, 3 eggs. Put butter in the saucepan first, then add the juice and grated rind of lemons, then beat up eggs and stir them in, continue stirring till it thickens, put into very light puff pastry tartlets, and only use quite fresh.

The platform café au lait, so dear to the memory of generations of travellers, should not be missed when available, for the dread experience of the crossing is behind, and the joys of a sunshine holiday await us; but in case the " dix minutes d'arrêt " prove but an insubstantial dream, this *Chelsea Bun* should be included in the basket, for it will be welcome alike in the cold dawn with a thermos of hot coffee, or with the etna and tea basket to enliven the long afternoon.

Chelsea Bun.

Half a pound flour, 5 oz. butter or margarine, 1 oz. sugar, pinch of salt, 3 eggs, $\frac{1}{2}$ oz. yeast. Mix the yeast with 2 oz. of the flour and a little tepid milk to make a light dough, place it to rise about 10 minutes. With the rest of the flour, put in sugar, eggs, and salt ; beat well together, then mix in melted butter ; then add the yeast, and work well together and stand in a cool place overnight. In the morning add the grated rind of a lemon or 2 small ones, a few sultanas, and some chopped peel. Form into a round on a baking sheet with a band of greased paper, brush over with egg, and stand in a warm place to rise

a little. Place in not too hot an oven,
and bake for about ½ hour.

A lemon or two slipped in for Chinese
Russian tea, together with a tin of peptonized
cocoa and milk, a tin of best consommé
capsules, some dried milk powder easily
mixed with water, a slab of first-rate chocolate
—these will provide hot drinks in variety.
Mineral waters and light wines are readily
procurable by the way, if space has forbidden
their inclusion at home. No experienced
traveller starts without a flask of brandy,
and the relative merits of biscuits (a matter
of personal preferences) are too well known
to need recalling. Fruit is of all forms of
refreshment the most wholesome and welcome on a journey, and the dried forms—
almonds and raisins, dates, and the crystallized varieties—are excellent and portable.

The travellers' food basket, equipped in
some such ways as are here suggested, will
render its owners independent of time and
place, fortified against hunger and thirst,
immune to the extortions and insolence of

officials, and they will be fresh and ready on arrival to enjoy the lovely sights and gay adventures awaiting them, for has it not been truly said : " We need all our sense to be aware of spirit " ?

XXV

FOR THE TOO THIN

MANY women of the present day are below their proper weight in relation to their age and height. With some this is the result of what our fashionable American friends call "*Starving for Shape*"; others object to eating many of the ordinary foods on grounds of principle or humanitarianism, so that, without pressing for specially cooked dishes, (an egotism many shrink from,) they frequently go without adequate nourishment. Both sexes often restrain their natural appetite for athletic reasons, wanting to ride, run, and dance light, and to excel in games and sports where weight is a handicap. Numbers of influenza convalescents, too, get reduced by illness, and their doctors will urge them "to feed up," "to put on weight," knowing by experience how excessive thinness induces nervous disorders with resultant neurasthenia.

The fattening properties of milk, farinaceous puddings, and sweets with Devonshire cream, of plenty of fresh butter with bread and potatoes, and of oatmeal, pulses, and cereals, of root vegetables and some fruits—these are too well known to require stressing. But inclination often fails, and fashion cries " Beware." A few attractive dishes are therefore suggested, hoping to make the observance of doctor's orders something of a pleasure as well as a duty, their niceness being, as it were, the smile on the face of the stern lawgiver.

Sardines à la Sackville.

Make a nice purée of potato a little moister than the ordinary mashed preparation ; place a thin layer, when cold, on an oblong silver or china dish ; cover this with a layer of sardines, boned and skinned ; mask this over with a thin coating of whipped cream ; place on this a further layer of mashed potato, more sardines, and cover over with the remainder of your shillingsworth of cream, whipped, peppered, and salted ; finish with a sprinkle of coralline red pepper and a few sprigs of surrounding watercress. With it send round Veda brown bread and butter. For a party of, say six, this potato mound might measure some 8 inches long by 5 inches wide and 2 to 3 inches deep. This is nice also for a summer luncheon first course, or a Sunday supper, and would be popular at a schoolroom high tea.

All the vegetable purée soups made with milk and butter are nourishing and flesh-making. Here is an excellent one slightly different from the usual type ; it was acquired during an enforced motor delay over supper-time at a small pension-farm on the Evian side of the Lake of Geneva.

For Potage Tapioca Mousseux.

Sprinkle into 1 pint veal stock about 2 dessertspoonfuls of fine tapioca such as Groults, and let it boil for 20 minutes. When ready to serve, slightly whip ¼ pint cream, pour it on to the soup, and whisk briskly till it all becomes frothy,

serving it at once from a brown glazed
soup tureen, well heated. Some milk
and the yolk of an egg could be substituted for cream, but disadvantageously.

This American way of serving *Chicken
à la Maryland* is good if the cook can de-
vote some time and care to it, and it has been
known to tempt a fugitive appetite.

Cut up a nice chicken in slices and
joints, season with black pepper plentifully, and leave for 4 hours. Dip in
a thin batter, and fry in butter till it
is a golden colour ; place it in a stewpan
with a pint of cream, letting it simmer
till the cream thickens. Serve with
hominy (or maizena) cake made by
boiling 1 pint milk with butter, pepper,
salt, and 3 tablespoonfuls of the maizena.
Slip in 1 whole egg and some grated
parmesan cheese after the hominy or
maizena is cooked. When cold, cut
out in half-moon shaped pieces ; egg,
bread-crumb, and fry these ; roast some
bananas, skin and halve them across, and
place round the chicken alternately with
the fritters. Pour the cream sauce
over the jointed pieces, and serve very
hot.

Perhaps the most fattening of all savouries is a marrow bone on toast. But it is probably more popular with men than with women—as, indeed, are most varieties of boiled and toasted cheese, which, being mixed with butter, help to put on weight. An original form of savoury is *Bonne Bouche Otello*, made out of a couple of large French plums to each guest, or a single Carlsbad plum. They must be softened by soaking in a little hot water ; one or two almonds, blanched and browned in melted butter and rolled in pepper, salt (and a little cayenne if liked hot) should be inserted in place of the extracted stone ; roll in a thin rasher of bacon and grill on a skewer. Have ready *croûtes* of fried bread, slip out the skewer, lay the little plum grills on them, and serve very hot.

For those who prefer sweets to savouries, this recipe for a *Bombe Caramel* should be gratefully received, the formula being a family secret generously communicated.

Take 6 yolks of eggs and 2 whites, 1 tablespoonful castor sugar, and whisk them over boiling water until warm ; withdraw and whip until cold, add a teacup of whipped cream, mix all together, put into a bombe mould, and freeze about 2 hours. When frozen scoop out centre, and fill with cold hard caramel made in the usual way and afterwards pounded and passed through a wire sieve. Sufficient for a pint mould for four persons. Serve with thin golden caramel sauce round and some crisp biscuits.

Lest these suggestions be considered too exacting in material or labour for some readers, a nice *Oatmeal Sunday Pudding* for family consumption is added.

Take 3 oz. coarse oatmeal, 3 oz. flour, 2 oz. butter (or margarine) $1\frac{1}{2}$ oz. sugar, rind of 1 lemon, $\frac{1}{2}$ teacupful treacle, $\frac{1}{2}$ teaspoonful carbonate of soda, $\frac{1}{2}$ teacupful milk, 2 oz. dried stoned and chopped raisins, ditto candied peel ; rub butter into flour, add oatmeal, sugar, soda, fruit, rind, and bind together with warmed milk and treacle. Turn into a greased mould or basin ; steam carefully for 2 or 3 hours. Turn out and serve with a sweet sauce or custard made hot.

The words inscribed on the Delphic Oracle, " Know thyself " and " Nothing too much," might well be written on our daily menu card, and in so far as they are observed will success and improvement accrue to the too thin.

XXVI

FOR THE TOO FAT

WE are reminded in Scripture that " All flesh is grass," but, as a great artist once added reassuringly, " We cannot be sufficiently thankful that all grass is not flesh." No one likes to be fat ; it is unbecoming, fatiguing, and impairs efficiency. And although the condition is oftener the result of defective metabolism than of undue or indiscriminate appetite, still the experience of the war years, with their scarcity of the flesh-making foods, shows that weight *can* be reduced by a diminished consumption of dairy produce, sugar, and starchy foods. Unfortunately, all the nicer things are on a weights and measures black list, and the annual advice of an eminent financial authority to " spend less " must be paraphrased into a diminished consumption of all nourishment for those who would grow thinner. The important drinking of sufficient fluid, moreover, should be transferred from meal times to a previous or subsequent hour. Such inconvenient advice is only acted on when it is given in return for payment by a medical expert, but there may possibly be some chance for a few gratuitous suggestions towards making an austere diet more varied and pleasurable than it often is.

Lemon Tea.

> For the early morning luxury, substitute 2 freshly-cut, thin slices of lemon, on to which boiling water has been poured. This, sipped from a delicate china cup, is fragrant and thinning.

If that insidious enemy, soup, be held indispensable at dinner, at least avoid the vegetable purées and bisques made with cream, butter, root vegetables, and rich fish, also the savoury potage in which milk and flour figure, and try clear *Consommé à l'Estragon*, with its delicate and clean flavour.

FOR THE TOO FAT

Make the required quantity of clear vegetable stock in the usual way, or use a chicken carcass or some veal, if convenient, with ordinary stock. For garnish pick and blanch some 6d. worth of tarragon, letting half simmer gently for 30 minutes in the consommé. About 10 minutes before dinner, whisk the whites of 2 eggs stiffly with salt and pepper, adding the rest of the tarragon leaves, dried and finely chopped ; take a heaped dessertspoonful of the whipped whites and drop each to the required number into a frying-pan of boiling water to poach for 3 minutes ; pour the boiling soup into a hot tureen, drain each poached white, and let them float like snow islands on the top, serving one to each person.

Natural Meat Jelly is made by slow simmering of a little good beef, and is nourishing and palatable. Served very cold as jelly with a rusk, or re-heated with a couple of diet biscuits, it makes an adequate and sustaining little meal.

To give variety to plain roast or grilled meat, serve with it in a brown oven-proof dish some fresh *Rognons Sautés*, blanched, freed from fat and skin, and cut into thin slices ; they only require cooking in stock thickened with a very little flour, and flavoured with wine, and mushroom, or tomato and chopped herbs. *Calves' Brains*, carefully washed and poached, can be served in the same sort of way from a white ramekin fireproof dish with a little *beurre noir* sauce mainly composed of diluted vinegar and lemon, a very little butter, and plenty of chopped parsley. This is good, too, with slightly devilled slices of lean meat. A *Salad à la Américaine*, made of the raw heart of a fresh young cabbage very finely shredded and diluted with some quite thin dressing made of raw yolks of eggs, and a little chili vinegar, served very cold, is a good accompaniment. Indeed, all green salads and many fruit ones may be used freely without risk of fattening, if dressed without rich sauce or abundant oil, lemon juice being substituted for vinegar for those of delicate digestion. A fresh or slightly pickled tongue is suitable food for those suffering from avoirdupoids, though still somewhat expensive. This recipe for the humbler *Braised Sheep's Tongues, Sauce Piquante*, could also be adapted to the larger ox tongue.

Place cut-up carrot, onion, celery, leeks in a stewpan with a walnut of butter, and put in number of tongues required; fry gently, turning the tongues, and add 1 cupful good stock, 1 bay leaf, thyme, and parsley. Let all braise gently for 3 hours, adding more stock as it reduces. Take out the tongues, skin and trim them, reduce the stock to a glaze and pour it through a strainer over the tongues, dish up on a bed of spinach, and serve with sauce made by cutting up 1 small onion fine, reducing it in a stewpan with 2 tablespoonfuls of vinegar till nearly dry; then add 1 small cup brown stock, 1 walnut-sized piece of glaze, 1 teaspoonful Harvey sauce, and let all boil. Finally add a few blanched almonds and a small quantity of orange peel, both cut into fine strips, or 2 tablespoonfuls unsweetened stoned cherries. A larger quantity of cherries could be warmed in clear gravy and served round the larger tongue if preferred.

Mixed Grills are another stand-by for anti-fat meals and can be pleasantly varied. A small chicken jointed, spread with tamarind preserve and grilled with an accompaniment of mushrooms ; mutton cutlets scored with chutney and grilled with tomato and chipolata sausages ; game of all kinds slightly devilled and sent round with a dish of green watercress, stewed soft, drained, finely chopped, moistened with stock, reheated, and just before serving a little lemon juice stirred in with pepper and salt.

For a winter dessert, try a black plum or two from a two-pound glass screw jar, after the top layer has been extracted and some cherry brandy poured in, adding more as the liqueur is absorbed by the plums, and keep it air-tight for two or three weeks before use.

Activities, mental and physical, play a large part in reducing weight, just as sloth and inertia promote it, for, in the words of Claudel, " Bien des choses se consument sur le feu d'un cœur qui brûle."

XXVII

SUNDAY SUPPER

SUNDAY hospitality is a problem which, in these days of diminished service and increased social activity, cannot be solved without forethought and tact. The kitchen and the pantry both claim and deserve consideration and some liberty ; but against this, relations and friends can often meet only at the week-ends, and drift hopelessly out of touch unless some point of contact is made pleasurable and easy. The lonely or hardworking bachelor, too, male or female (for the term has come to include both sexes), is specially grateful for Sunday welcome, and inspiration for the future as well as sympathy in past and present interests are oftenest sought and found on " the day which comes between a Saturday and Monday."

KITCHEN ESSAYS

Sometimes a group of relations or friends can evolve a system of mutual hospitality; but all inelastic bands are apt to snap disagreeably, and any feeling of obligation is ruinous to spontaneous companionship. Of late the restaurant has often had to solve the difficulty; but, except for a *tête-à-tête*, this can hardly be considered a general solution, if purse, health, or privacy are to count. Rather let adequate provision, made beforehand, liberate as many workers as possible, and the well-furnished side-tables, where each can supply individual needs with little or no service, give a sense of freedom and informality which will compensate for any slight diminution of comfort. If the number of guests be known and limited, a cold meat course might be attractively presented for each one in some such fashion as this: Purchase or cut thin slices, circular as the base of the dinner plates, off a rolled and spiced round of beef, or long slices off a brick of cold pressed beef; ally with it a slice of tongue or ham, and pour over both

a thin sheet of well-flavoured aspic jelly—
some attractive bits of lettuce or watercress
and a gay radish or two, cut into rosy-edged
slices and imprisoned in the jelly. This
will make an inviting supper. Alternatively,
some pieces of white boiled chicken in béchamel on a *mousse* made of their own
less delicate parts not wholly devoid perhaps
of some purée of foie gras, with pale aspic
chopped small, and green beans, peas, or
quarters of tomato as a garnish ; or, best of
all, with the half of an American pickled
peach and some salad. If pickled peaches
are considered extravagant—as, alas ! they
are—a good substitute can be made with
the best quality of evaporated apricots,
well steeped and softened in clove-flavoured
water and treated with a little vinegar or
lemon and a few drops of brandy or liqueur.
These are good also as fruit salad with any
cold meats. Cold ducks stuffed with a
delicate *mousse*, cold chickens stuffed with
rice made savoury with tomato or pimentoes,
or an uncut leg of lamb set round with

little jelly castles of mint sauce made with aspic and chopped mint — these, together with a bowl of appetizing potato salad, will deprive the visitor's bell of half its terrors, and the impetuous hospitalities of irresponsible youth might then pass uncensured.

Potato Salad.

Take kidney or the most waxy potatoes obtainable, boil in their skins, peel while warm, cut into thickish slices, pour on 1 tablespoonful vinegar and about 2 tablespoonfuls stock, but very gradually so that they may absorb it ; add 2 tablespoonfuls oil, some pepper and salt to taste, and 1 small finely-chopped onion, and let it all stand for an hour before serving. A very, very thin mayonnaise sauce with a little French mustard and a drop or two of garlic vinegar, and a few capers with parsley and chives may be used as an alternative dressing.

This cold *Mousse of Whiting and Lobster* (for six) is a nice supper or warm weather luncheon dish.

Boil 2 good-sized whitings, and when

cold pass through a fine wire sieve with a little cold salmon, and put it into a basin with salt, pepper, cream, and half a teacup of liquid aspic jelly; thoroughly mix. Line a brick-shaped or charlotte mould with aspic; when set put in a layer of lobster cut in small pieces, then half fill with the fish *mousse*, then another layer of lobster, and fill up the mould with the rest of the fish; pour over a layer of aspic, and leave to set. Turn out, and serve with a cucumber, beet-root, or other salad, with green sand-wiches of brown bread and butter and a bowl of mayonnaise sauce.

Attractive sweets are always easy to make or procure, and the simpler ones—such as *macédoines* of fruit with a Devonshire junket or creamy rice, or méringues, or a bowl of orange jelly, or trifles—are hard to beat, but a *Chocolate Marrée* or an *Open French Tart* might have for some the glamour of a new acquaintance which could ripen into friendship. For the first, take ¼ lb. of the best chocolate *à la vanille* you can find or afford. Let it steam over a stewpan of boiling water for 30 minutes ; then gradually work into it 4 raw yolks of eggs till smooth ; whisk the whites to a stiff froth, and mix all together lightly. Pour into a shallow round glass dish, and let it stand 12 hours, and serve cold and white with 6d. of fresh cream poured all over it, and these *Vanilla Crescents* in attendance. Take 2 oz. each of sifted sugar, fresh butter, ground almonds, pastry flour, and a pinch of baking powder, a little salt, a bit of vanilla pod scraped. Mix all into paste; make some cords 5 to 6 inches long and thick as a middle finger, and shape them into flattish horseshoes. Cover with white sugar, and bake in a moderately hot oven for 20 minutes.

For the flat *Tart :*

Line the bottom of a round fireproof or oven glass dish with good short pastry; bake a golden brown. When cold spread with a liberal layer of lemon cheese mixture; on the top of this a layer of home-made raspberry jam, and cover all with some slightly-whipped cream.

But at Sunday supper it often matters less what is on the table than what is on the chairs; and if these are fortunately furnished, preceding suggestions could be disregarded, and " a loaf of bread, a jug of wine," might be found entirely adequate provision.

XXVIII

OF WEDDING BREAKFASTS

MARRIAGE feasts resemble the institution
they celebrate, of which Montaigne observed
that those within its confines often struggled
to get out, whilst those without endeavoured
to get in. When the human contents of
a spacious church are transferred into the
few rooms of an average dwelling, the laws
of the container and the contained are set
at naught, and we shall agree with Arago
that "He is a rash man who pronounces the
word 'Impossible' anywhere, even within
the sphere of pure mathematics."

Those whose tribal instincts and gre-
garious tastes necessitate a long invitation
list, may endeavour to reduce the ultimate
crush (and not without success) by prelimi-
nary tea-parties and an evening reception;

but a large proportion of guests will nevertheless attend on the wedding day, either because they enjoy the human drama, or fear lest their defection be counted unfriendly. Some few, of tried adoption, genuinely concerned in the fortunes of the adventurers, will wish to see the ship successfully launched on its uncharted voyage. Yet of all the actions of a man's life, his marriage least concerns other people, and it is ever the one most meddled with.

Wedding breakfasts in town are now generally reduced to the conventional stand-up buffet provided from outside, where choices of tea and coffee, hot or iced, of wine-cups and lemonades, of sandwiches and stuffed rolls, fancy cakes, ices, and some easily consumed sweet dishes are all that are expected, provided the appointments be dainty, the quality perfect, and the service dexterous. This recipe for *Iced Jelly* (for eight) may be suitable for any occasion when the guests are warm, the dishes cold.

Boil 2 calves' feet for several hours, strain off and leave to get cold. Remove all grease, and put them into a stewpan with the peel and juice of 4 lemons to each quart of liquor, ½ lb. loaf sugar, a piece of cinnamon stick and a few raisins, the whites of 4 eggs. Whisk all well together whilst boiling ; strain through a jelly bag several times until clear. Flavour liberally with a sherry glass of maraschino, pour into an ice mould with secure lid, pack in ice and freezing salt in an ice pail, and freeze for 2 hours. Serve with a silver knife to cut it, and a bowl of fruit *macédoine*. The inner core should be firm and amber-coloured, the outside shell of a paler and more frozen consistency. Ordinary lemon jelly with sherry flavouring may be advantageously iced in the same way.

Biscuits Tuiles are a pleasant addition to ices or fruit :—

Take 3 oz. each of flour, white sugar, melted butter, 3 whites of eggs partly whipped, a little vanilla essence, 3 oz. chopped almonds. Mix together, place in small rounds on greased baking sheet, leaving room to spread. Bake golden brown, remove quickly on to a rolling-pin to dry and curl over.

Here also is a recipe for *Punche à la Romaine*, offered in the hope that it may be of service for celebrating some marriage day or great festival occasion.

> Take 1½ pint orange and lemon syrup mixed, 1 pint champagne, ½ pint rum, ½ cup green tea, 4 whites of eggs whipped and stirred in gradually. It should be frozen soft, not hard, and served in wine glasses, either before, half-way through, or at the end of dinner.

The far-seeing parent will ensure a quick and tactful luncheon for the bride and bridegroom, in a room apart, with perhaps two or three favoured companions—some vitalizing consommé, a casserole of chicken with potatoes and peas, some dainty sweet or delicious fruit, and the drinks of their choice, would be suitable provision, and from this repast they must hasten to rejoin their guests and open the attack on that romantic survival, the wedding cake.

KITCHEN ESSAYS

Country weddings must often take place
early in the day, and so necessitate a more
substantial sitting-down meal for everybody,
small tables supplementing the large ceremonial one where are gathered the guests of
honour. There the complicated foods we
are so erroneously supposed to like, and so
seldom do, are offered in bewildering variety;
and mayonnaises, mousses, aspics, succeeded
by elaborate creams, jellies, pastries, and or-
namental cakes, appear in profusion, whilst
confidential butlers pour champagne encour-
agingly into frugal glasses as the anxious
moment for speeches draws near. Might it
not be better to concentrate effort and
expenditure on two or three really first-
rate dishes of universal acceptance? Sil-
very salmon or sea trout, lobsters fresh
from their rocky homes, peach-fed hams,
abundant chickens hot, young, and undis-
guised, crisp lettuces, and perfect potatoes;
compotes of fruit with generous bowls of
whipped cream, cakes of the best, but not
masquerading as flowers or towering into

castellated buildings, all these would be welcome !

In both types of wedding breakfasts there is a tendency towards the conventional, the stereotyped, unworthy of this greatest day in life.

" Rarely comest thou, Spirit of Delight ! " And what wonder, seeing the conditions of our welcome ! If, instead of the refreshment caterer with his contract properties, Beauty's daughters were to prepare the feast, how lovely it might be and what a pleasure ground for memory ! A table spread with white and gold brocade, a room hung with garlands of myrtle and bay, and generous sheaves of the perfect bridal flowers—roses, lilies and magnolias, tulips, carnations and orange blossom— all in their seasons. Great dishes and platters of silver and gold, or gleaming brass, piled high with fruits—peaches and grapes, pineapples and plums, oranges, apples, melting pears—flagons of red wine, goblets of sparkling drink, delicious fragrance of rosemary, lavender, and cedar wood in all the air—unseen voices singing madrigals, music, laughter, and the love of friends. What an hour to remember later in the silence and the starlight.

We are a warm-hearted and sentimental people for all our so-called British phlegm, as was shown by the spontaneous rejoicing and sympathy evoked by a recent royal wedding, when a whole nation, as it seemed, were unseen well-wishers at the feast.

Even the most critical and cold-hearted must feel something of the dramatic solemnity of the rite and pass in silent review their own lives, so chequered with hopes, memories, and regrets. For always the Institution of Marriage can be, not only what the Prayer Book says it is, but also the means of enabling the happy and the fortunate to deal with many difficult matters, and to do many lovely charities for those less blessed than themselves, for the doing of which two heads and two hearts are—not better than—but the perfection of one.

XXIX

THEIR FIRST DINNER-PARTY

THE first dinner-party is always an interesting event in a newly-founded home, and should be so organized as not to monopolize the attention of host and hostess to the exclusion of social enjoyment. It must not err on the side of parsimony, nor yet by its lavishness vex those new relations or old aunts whose attitude has been aptly characterized as " affectionate, but hostile." " Not fewer in number than the Graces, nor yet exceeding the Muses," runs an old adage regarding the perfect party; so, avoiding both danger points, let the table be well and truly laid for eight cheerful guests. All beginnings are important. If you can establish a name for having good food by a series of successful hospitalities, friends will grow lyrical over

your cold mutton, and even ask for the recipe
of the Shepherd's Pie—so potent and mysterious are the workings of suggestion ! On
that principle oysters or caviare might well
be ordered to head the first menu, but they
are costly additions, and, as George Meredith
was wont to say, " Economy, our dread old
friend, must decide ! "

Clear soup gives the cook her first chance,
and already a dress rehearsal will have given
a taste of its quality. Having attained to a
well-flavoured consommé, cut some carrots,
onions, celery, turnips, into very small dice,
if for a *Brunoise;* and into fine strips with
the green parts of leeks added, if for *Julienne.*
Cook these slowly to a golden colour in plenty
of butter for an hour (the butter does again
for similar purposes), and sprinkle them
lightly with white sugar. Drain them dry,
put them into the simmering consommé,
and let them gently cook for from 1½ to 2
hours. Skim off any grease before serving.

The fish course must be chosen with
reference to the market and the special apti-

tude of the cook. *Filets de Soles à la Creme*, *Pommes Pailles*, is safe, choosing medium soles, one to every four guests, the fillets nicely trimmed and put into a buttered oven-proof dish with seasoning, and covered with buttered paper.

> Cook for 10 minutes and fold together, dishing with some of their own liquor mixed with some heated cream poured over them, on a long hot metal dish, potato straws of the length and thickness of the smallest wax match, well dried before immersion in very hot lard and drained dry afterwards, heaped at either end, and sprinkled along the edges. A sauce boat with a good mousseline sauce could be added, and in that case the fillets should be served less moist.

For the *pièce de résistance* a very small *Selle de Pré Sâle* (Saddle of Welsh Mutton) in winter ; in spring a tiny saddle of English lamb would be hard to beat. That any reproach of dullness may be taken away, treat it thus :—

For a saddle weighing about 8 lb. take

some 6 lb. of turnips; when cooked
squeeze through a cloth to get out all the
water; mix with a little stiff white sauce
or thick cream, add pepper and salt, make
very hot, carve the saddle into long thin
slices as required for number of guests,
fill the space so cleared on either side
with the purée of creamed turnip, replace the slices crosswise above it, pour
over a little very hot gravy. The kidneys, taken out before roasting the
saddle, and cut into rounds, fried with
their fat left on, can be served on or
about the saddle, or sharing a long dish
with new or purée potatoes, together
with the other vegetables chosen, and
followed by a bowl of red currant jelly
or mint sauce. A nicely-prepared vegetable course might be interpolated after
the roast; peas *à la Française*, or asparagus with hollandaise sauce, would
be the most popular selection.

For a sweet, choose *Crêmes Glacées Tutti
Frutti*, taking for eight persons :—

One pint of cream; add 1 dessertspoonful each of curaçoa, maraschino,
and rum. Whip until light; serve in
small glasses, preferably like the small
size of Pyrex round glasses, wider at

the top than the bottom ; allow sufficient cream for each portion, and freeze
in the ice cave for 1½ hour. Before
serving, lay round the edges a gay but
narrow ruching of finely-cut crystallized
fruits, an apricot, greengage, pink pear,
red cherries, all shredded, mixed, and
saturated with the same liqueurs ; tea-
spoons on the dish between each glass
and small fresh home-made macaroon
biscuits to accompany.

A ripe camembert, with hot oat-cakes,
crisp water biscuits, and well-iced butter may
be preferred to a savoury ; for dessert one
dish of the most beautiful fruits in season
mingled in picturesque variety ; choose also
carefully those sweets men often affect to
disdain but more frequently enjoy. The
wines, cigars, coffee, and liqueurs must all
be as good as you can afford, and the *Barley
Water*—for many guests like an alternative
drink—should be cold and plentiful, but
restrained as to sugar and lemon juice.

Here is a recipe often greeted as perfect ;
but barley water can, like coffee, a spring

day, and a charming woman, produce miracles
of variety out of the same constituents :—

> Wash three tablespoonfuls of pearl bar-
> ley in a quart of water two or three times
> changed and thrown away. Put a fresh
> quart of water with the barley, bring
> to the boil, simmer slowly for 10 min-
> utes. Strain into a jug, add juice of
> 2 lemons, sugar to taste, and set on ice
> till wanted. Enough for three or four.

Having given of your best, inevitable criti-
cism must be borne with philosophy, remembering the motto inscribed on the walls of
a certain ancient Scottish college : " They
say— What say they ?—Let them say ! "

XXX

MEATLESS MEALS

A CERTAIN *maigre* luncheon on a sunny
Friday of an early summer, now far away
and long ago, was vividly impressed on the
mind of one of the party of four who enjoyed
it, partly because of the beauty of its setting
and the stimulating interest of the talk in
that brief hour of refection, but also because
of the discovery that such very simple things
could be so much better than the elaborate
and expensive ones which often complicate
the sweet uses of hospitality The garden
room of an educational institution set amongst
those lovely wooded hills which dip to the
sea near Dublin, a Jesuit father of great in-
tellectual distinction and goodness, a nun
with a " divine plain face," and two searchers
after truth—this the scene and the party.

219

Never before had newly-laid eggs scrambled
so deliciously with young asparagus, or pink-
fleshed trout tasted so fresh in the company
of tiny potatoes and crisp lettuce. A whole-
meal loaf and milk scones were there, with
home-made cream cheese ; the first fruits
of the bee-hive also, tasting of the scent of
lime trees in blossom, and the last fruits of
the dairy in golden butter. Woodland strawberries, harbingers of the summer, in leaf-
lined baskets, gave out their fugitive aroma,
and finally a brown jug of coffee freshly
roasted and ground, hot and fragrant beyond
all previous experience, brought its valedic-
tory blessing to a perfect meal. How gross
in comparison appeared the joints of butcher's meat, the slaughtered game and poultry
of daily life, until the great reconciler, custom,
should blunt afresh our susceptibilities !
Since meatless days are the rule of many at
certain Church seasons, and of many more
at all seasons, some suggestions for making
maigre menus more generally acceptable to
all may not come amiss ; for did not Mary

MEATLESS MEALS

Coleridge remind us in a pleasant volume of table talk that " Self-sacrifice is the noblest thing in the world, but to sacrifice other people, even for a noble thing, is as wrong as persecution."

Here is a breakfast or high-tea notion for a busy worker on a long winter's day, when time and thoughts race too quickly for more deliberate nourishment : A crumpet with lots of butter and salt ; on it an egg, or maybe two, perfectly fried, the pepper-mill just going out of action, and all served piping hot in a warmed muffin dish. This is moderate in cost, simple in preparation, nourishing, and nice.

Here are two soups of proved excellence— one for coast dwellers or those near a good fish-market, and owning a well-filled purse ; the other for everyman and everywhere. For a restrained and anglicized *Bouillabaisse* for four—

> Make about a quart of fish stock in the usual way, with the trimmings, bones, and shell of the fish and lobster to be

used subsequently. Cut up 2 large onions, and fry them in ½ gill of Lucca oil, add a teaspoonful of flour, a tumbler of white wine, pepper, salt, a fagot of parsley, a bay leaf, and 3 tablespoonfuls of tomato sauce. Boil from 15 to 20 minutes, pass through sieve, and return to saucepan. Cut up a small lobster into pieces, also a gurnet, bream, or flounder, of which the trimmings have been already utilized, for the fish stock. Boil ½ hour on a quick fire with the prepared stock, put a slice of bread, or preferably several small slices from a French roll, into a warmed tureen, transfer the fish with a strainer on to the bread, pour the broth over all, and serve together. When time is a considera‑ tion, as before some evening perfor‑ mance, this portmanteau of two courses is useful.

Everyman Soup, for four persons.

Melt in a stewpan 1½ oz. butter, stir into it smoothly 2 tablespoonfuls *crême de riz* flour. Add 1 quart milk (or if permissible, some light veal stock and milk mixed); let it cook for 10 minutes. Then add 2 tablespoonfuls freshly-grated parmesan or other cheese, and some pieces of macaroni previously washed and boiled in milk and cut into ¼-inch sections ; or get some of those small shell-shaped Italian pastes called *coquilli* procurable fresh in Soho. Just before serving, pour the boiling soup on to a yolk of egg mixed with a little cream ; stir all smooth, and pour into a hot marmite pot.

Clever *maigre* combinations of eggs, fish, vegetables, and fruit give abundant scope for culinary talent. Try for a useful luncheon dish :—

Œufs Mollets. Sauce Fromage.
Boil your finest eggs soft inside, firm when peeled and skinned ; balance them on circlets of fried bread within a low rampart of dry boiled rice ; send them round with a bowl of bubbling hot cheese sauce made by stirring into a pint of nicest thin béchamel a ¼ lb. grated cheddar ; to be ladled out over the eggs and rice.

If your cook has the puff-pastry touch, a *Vol-au-Vent* case confers distinction on all manner of noble relics, united in the bonds of a good sauce. Sea-kale boiled tender in milk and cut into short lengths, and diluted with béchamel, varieties of haricot beans, mildly curried and mixed with cauliflower, remains of fish with lobster or shrimp sauce, and, best of all, creamed oysters, will compose suitable fillings if skilfully treated.

Thatched House Pudding.

This old country-house favourite is really too nice for Lenten fare, but it could give opportunities for self-denial, and might come in usefully at any season. It is worth rehearsing into perfection if the first attempt should prove a little uncertain. Melt 2 oz. butter, add 4 tablespoonfuls flour. Pour in enough boiling milk to the consistence of a hasty pudding ; add yolks of 4 eggs and grated rind of 1 lemon, with a little juice and sugar to taste. Whisk the whites stiffly, and add to the mixture. Put all in an oven-proof dish (a Pyrex glass one, $10\frac{1}{2}$ inches by $6\frac{1}{2}$ inches by 2 inches, just holds this quantity for six or seven). Cook from 15 to 20 minutes. Before serving and after it has risen, pour over the top a cupful of hot thin apricot jam, and sprinkle with a liberal ounce of browned and chopped almonds.

With so many good things for meatless menus to choose from, our thoughts need never turn to what we lack, but rather find contentment in all we have.

XXXI

ON SAVOURIES

SOME people abstain from sweets at certain seasons, on grounds of religion or health, but seek compensation for their self-denial in tasty savouries ; others never eat sweets because they dislike them, but expect something to replace them ; and by many a dinner which does not include both sweet and savoury is thought, even in these days of shortened meals, to be a little disappointing. A few suggestions, then, as to savouries may not come amiss, though in France, that spiritual home of the great artists in cookery, a savoury course intervening between a sweet and dessert is looked on as something barbarous, indeed almost immoral. Morality, however, as Samuel Butler reminds us in his often startling note-books, " is the

custom of one's country, and the current
feeling of one's peers ; so that cannibalism
is quite moral in a cannibal country."

Our lusty forefathers liked their savouries
hot and strong, and *Toasted Cheese*, redolent
of mustard and beer, bubbled its way down
the long tables, a red-hot iron glowing
within its pewter serving-dish. Nowadays,
fireproof china or the chafing-dish solve the
question of service, and there should be no
excuse for its not hissing into the dining-
room, with a forerunner of freshly-made
hot toast. There are many good recipes,
but this is a favourite for a savoury dear
to those who have dined lightly and can
slumber deep. For six people, allow about
6 oz. of a good toasting cheese, single
Gloucester or mature cheddar ; shred it
finely, and mix it with a breakfastcupful of
good white sauce, made with milk, butter,
and a very little flour in the usual way.
Stir this over the fire till the cheese is
melted and smoothly incorporated, let it boil,
pour it into a heated white china oblong

fireproof eared dish, and serve whilst still bubbling and seething together with mustard and hot toast. Toasted cheese is apt to be stringy and tough if undiluted.

A nice savoury of *Oysters au Gratin* can be made by serving two or three hot on a scallop shell with their own moisture, and a tiny grilled roll of bacon above some buttered bread-crumbs, a squeeze of lemon, and a taste of cayenne completing the preparation before a lightning transit from fire to table.

Marrow Bones with hot toast and lots of pepper, though ogre's food, are too good not to be sometimes invited to the party; but let them appear rarely, and in the absence of the sensitive.

These *Croûtes de Laitance* make an excellent savoury.

Serve the hot soft herring-roes moistened with milk or butter on long thin narrow strips of well-made and nicely-browned puff pastry, about 6 inches by 2 inches; if the herring-roes are small, allow two, overlapping, to each person; a light dusting of coralline pepper is an im-

provement. This also makes a nice first
course luncheon dish.
A hot toast spread with some anchovy-
flavoured butter or paste and covered
with several roes, and the white of an
egg stiffly whisked and flung on it for
a moment before it leaves the fire, is a
homely savoury for a cosy dinner of two.

Little puff-pastry boats made in small
moulds sold for the purpose came into
fashion for dinner-party savouries recently,
and can be filled with all manner of cargo,
such as eggs scrambled with cheese, or cold,
hard-boiled, and chopped with a little gherkin and capers ; sardines made into a purée
beneath a thin veil of soufflé mixture, or
of savoury custard, slightly browned in
the oven ; anchovies beaten with cream
into a cold cayenne flavoured *mousse*, coming chilled from the refrigerator with a thin
sprinkle of cress ; but beware of over-elaboration.

The least complicated savouries are often
the best, and caviare or slices of foie gras,
ice-cold with hot toast, or hot truffles *en*

serviette with ice-cold butter, or thin slices of smoked salmon with brown and white bread and butter are the gourmet's choice, although few fortunes or consciences are sufficiently robust in these days for luxuries so costly.

A novel and successful savoury was evolved the other day thus, and called *Croûtes aux Prunes Farcies*.

> Make nice little *canapés* of fried bread, about 2 inches by 3 inches, 1 for each person ; take the biggest French plum procurable (or 2), soak it and extract the stone ; fill the cavity with a stuffing of Scotch dried haddock, cooked, flaked, and beaten with a little cream and red pepper to a smooth *mousse* serve hot.

Mushrooms are useful for savouries, but great care must be exercised in their selection, and any stale or doubtful ones rejected. American cuisine has invented special Pyrex glass saucers with bell glasses fitting over them, in which mushrooms are cooked very

simply with salt, pepper, cream, and butter,
so as to retain their juices and fugitive
flavour ; but this might be thought too pro-
fuse a savoury for the end of a varied dinner,
when these little *Croûtes de Champignons*
would be considered daintier.

> Make a purée by frying about ½ lb.
> mushrooms, or steaming them, in some
> butter. When cooked, pass through
> a wire sieve, mix with a little stiff
> béchamel sauce, salt, and pepper, heap
> this on some fried or toasted croutons
> of bread, and on the top of each little
> mound place a small whole grilled mush-
> room and serve very hot.

Unsweetened wafer biscuits with grated
cheese flaked liberally on to them and served
very hot from the grill, also hot thin water
biscuits spread with a savoury dressing of
grated cheese and mustard, with flavouring
of Worcester or Harvey sauce, and sent round
with a cold cream cheese and celery or cress,
will be counted amongst the best preludes
to a good glass of wine. Perhaps it is as

well that we live in our desires rather than in our achievements, and if the ideal savoury has still to be discovered, many ambitious cooks can use their brains and skill in its elusive pursuit

XXXII

FOOD FOR THE PUNCTUAL AND THE UNPUNCTUAL

IN a delightful chapter in Plutarch's Lives describing the home life of Anthony, Lampryas tells of his visit to the kitchen, where he saw " a world of diversities of meats, amongst them eight wild boars roasting whole, and wonderful sumptuous preparations for one supper." When he inquired as to the number of guests expected the cook fell a-laughing and said : " Not above twelve in all, yet all must be served in whole or it might be marred, for Antoninus peradventure will sup presently, or it may be a pretty while hence, or likely enough he will defer it long, for he hath drunken well to-day, or he may have some great matters in hand ; and therefore we do not dress *one*

233

supper only, but *many* suppers, because we are uncertain of the hour he will sup in."

He is a bold man who would call on his cook for such devotion and elasticity in these days !

In unjust contrast this passage from Hawkesworth's Life of Dr. Swift shows what can befall a punctual and deserving master : " The dean had a kitchen wench for his cook, a woman of a large size, robust constitution and coarse features, her face very much seamed with the smallpox and furrowed by age ; this woman he always distinguished by the name ' Sweetheart.' It happened one day that ' Sweetheart ' greatly over-roasted the only joint he had for dinner ; upon which he sent for her, and with great coolness and gravity : ' Sweetheart,' says he, ' take this down into the kitchen and do it less.' She replied that was impossible ' Pray, then,' said he, ' if you had roasted it too little, could you have done it more ? ' ' Yes,' she said, easily could she have done that. ' Why, then, Sweetheart,' replied the dean, ' let me advise you, if you must commit a fault, commit a fault that can be mended.' "

The punctual and the unpunctual are always with us, so it is a wise cook who knows her own master, and in preparing dinner she may like to make choice of these few suggestions according to the measure of her hope or her experience.

For the Punctual. *Poulet Grillé Saint Jean.*

Bone a nice chicken, or, if a novice, let it be boned at the purveyor for future imitation. Prepare a farce from veal or the best parts of a rabbit in the usual way, with ½ teacupful cream, 1 whole egg, and seasoning added to the pounded meat. Fill the inside of the boned bird, which will be spread out flat, with the farce, and cook under the gas or electric griller. Serve it, preferably, on a silver-plated grill above a meat dish, or on a long fireproof dish, cut right across in thick 1 inch slices, with perfectly-made bread-sauce, gravy, and a garnish of watercress, or a cold Tartar sauce if preferred.

Soufflé de Prunes à la Russe.

Boil ½ lb. French plums till soft, rub through a hair sieve, keep the purée soft and moist ; whisk into it by degrees whilst hot 6 whites of eggs. Fill the mixture into a low plated dish and bake for 10 minutes in a sharp oven. Send up with some vanilla iced cream served separately, or some small blobs of stiffly-whipped cream dropped on the top of the soufflé as it goes in.

For the Unpunctual, try a savoury dish of *Papprika*, thus :—

Skin 4 large onions, cut up, and stew them a bright golden colour with 6 oz. fresh butter. Rub this through a fine sieve with ½ pint sour cream, a salt-spoonful of salt, ½ teaspoonful Papprika pepper (procurable at all Stores), and add your previously jointed and cooked chicken, or slices of cooked meat, game, or rabbit ; let this heat thoroughly and slowly ; serve in a casserole with plain boiled rice, slightly flavoured with Papprika, and a green vegetable.

236

Iced Chicken Soufflé with Curried Livers.

Pound the breast of a boiled chicken, adding ½ pint béchamel sauce, and pass it through a hair sieve. Whip ½ pint cream ; add it to the chicken. Take a white fireproof soufflé dish, stand a small jar in the centre, filling the soufflé dish around with the chicken cream. Set it in the ice cave for some 2 hours. Remove jar and fill in the space with 6 or 8 curried chicken livers, trimmed, and put in a stewpan with a walnut of butter, and seasoning. Cook these for some 10 minutes ; add 1 teaspoonful each of curry powder, curry paste, and 1 tablespoonful desiccated cocoanut (previously steeped and stirred in hot milk and most of the nut part eliminated) and a little chopped shallot. Let the livers cook in this for another 10 minutes to absorb most of the moisture before letting them get cold and adding to the chicken soufflé. With this serve cold curried rice and brown bread-and-butter sandwiches with a little chutney in them.

For a long-suffering sweet, try this *Apricot Purée*.

Stew 1 lb. best evaporated apricots

after an all-night soak. When cooked soft, add a small tin of peeled apricots ; boil together, sweetening to taste ; reduce the syrup, pass through a wire sieve, and put into a shallow glass bowl ; cover completely with a thin layer of partly-whipped cream (about 6d. worth), and perhaps a few chopped pistachio nuts to embellish. With this send round a glass finger-bowl of that useful American cereal " puffed rice " just crisped in the oven, to be sprinkled on by each guest. This sweet is suitable also for holiday luncheons or Sunday suppers.

" It is better to be punctual than to be sorry," is an admonition that has often embarrassed apologetic youth ; but fortunately women are by nature forgiving, and the erring often more lovable than the faultless.

XXXIII

HINTS FOR HOLIDAY HOUSEKEEPING

THERE are any number of reasons for leaving home for an Easter holiday, and all of them good. Many of us, like blind Milton, " have been long in populous city pent, where houses thick and sewers annoy the air," and the scent of primrose-starred woods and budding larches can intoxicate even our imaginations. Breadwinners who have worked hard need fresh air and exercise. Children who have wintered and schooled in town hear the call of Spring with longing, and should not be denied its short-lived rapture ; whilst mistress and maids alike demand the opportunity for an annual purification of the dwelling after the long dirt-dealing months of winter. We must not, however, forget

that those who preside over seaside quarters
or farmhouse rooms, or the caretakers of our
country cottages may hold narrow views of
holidaymakers' requirements, and often dis-
appoint the most legitimate claims, the most
reasonable expectations. " We never provide anything hot after the mid-day meal,
and we don't look to do any cooking of a
Sunday," is a not infrequent lodging-house
formula ; and even those things we might
expect the country to provide in easy profusion are often strangely absent. Fresh
fish is notoriously unprocurable along the
coasts, chickens and vegetables only materi-
alize in streets and Stores, and milk, cream,
and butter are rare in those rural surroundings
where they should most abound. The wise
housekeeper will, then, prepare a hamper at
home wherewith to satisfy country appetites
and equip holiday excursions, thus precluding
friction or disappointment. Let her pack a
case from her own storeroom, or select one
from some of the great Stores who deliver
free, unless local enterprise can be relied on

to provide her adequately. She might include some good jam, and a few favourite biscuits such as gingerbread-nuts, Scotch shortbreads, and digestive whole-meals. A loaf cheddar, a sugar-glazed ham and a pickled tongue, together with a home-made game-pie will be invaluable. Some potted fish, tinned fruits and vegetables, a case of oranges, lemons, and apples, some raisins, dates, first-rate chocolate and peppermint sweets, with a little choice tea, coffee, and cocoa, and home, sweet home will still be loved, but not regretted. As tea will probably be the first meal, here is a good big *Dundee Cake* made at home to enrich it.

> Cream together 1 lb. each fresh butter and castor sugar, add the grated rind of a lemon ; then one by one beat in 8 eggs and beat all for 10 minutes, then work in $1\frac{1}{4}$ lb. flour with a teaspoonful of baking powder mixed in ; then add $1\frac{1}{2}$ lb. sultanas, $\frac{1}{2}$ lb. mixed peel ; put in buttered cake tin, sprinkle the top liberally with blanched almonds, and bake in a moderate oven for $2\frac{1}{2}$ hours.

Lemon Marmalade

is easily made and gives welcome variety from the more trusted companion of the breakfast table. Cut some good lemons as for marmalade. To each lemon allow ¾ lb. sugar, ¾ pint water. After the lemons are cut up, allow to stand in the required quantity of water for 24 hours. Then add in the sugar, and boil in the usual way as for marmalade, until the syrup jellies. This is better used fresh, and made in small quantities.

Game Pie.

Two pounds of calf's liver, 2 lb. not very fat bacon cut into squares, a walnut piece of butter, pepper, salt, and spices, parsley and shallot finely chopped. Fry these gently together. When cooked put them into a mortar, after first removing the fat, pound well, and season highly. Bone and skin a chicken, or rabbit, or game, cut into moderate-sized pieces and fry in a stewpan with butter. Do not brown it. When cooked firm but tender, season with allspice and black pepper. Lay some of the pounded forcemeat at the bottom of a large oval game pie-dish, cover with a layer of chicken or game, mixing the white and brown meat, and so on till dish is full, ending with a top layer of forcemeat. Put this game pie-dish into a stewpan half-full of water on the fire for 2 or 3 hours, according to size. When cooked press contents tightly down and round the dish and flatten with a wooden spoon. Pour clarified butter thinly over the top to exclude air ; garnish with broken aspic and parsley.

Potted Salmon is a popular adjunct to high tea, and can be home-made thus :—

Boil 1 lb. fresh salmon. When cold pound it well in a mortar with 2 oz. fresh butter, a little pounded mace, salt, and a pinch of cayenne ; pass through a wire sieve, adding a little more butter if too stiff ; press well down in a potted meat jar and cover over with some clarified butter.

If you have included some American sweet corn in your tinned vegetables, it can be easily heated, and used as a ground-work for a nice supper-dish of poached eggs. If a simple sweet for young children easily made upstairs is desired, try what Chinese cooks delight to offer as *Engleesh Strawberry*

Mash—namely, skinned bananas cut up and mashed with strawberry jam into a thick moist purée, and served in a glass bowl with thick cream over the top. Should there be any ice handy—but no, that is the thought of an optimist ; yet, eaten with eyes shut, it will recall the 4th of June to Etonians, and many a garden tea-party in lovely summer. When the young people have gone to bed, a tiny glass of this *Orange Cordial* from the storeroom would not come amiss. Take 4 selected lemons and 4 Seville oranges ; peel very thin and slice finely into a large crock (with cover) with 1½ lb. loaf sugar broken small. To this add ½ gallon unsweetened gin and halfpennyworth of hay saffron. Let this stand 8 days in a warm place, stirring it once a day. Strain and bottle. This should make three bottles.

Any omissions in the commissariat will provide valuable guidance for the future, and there are few places and occasions where an open mind cannot acquire some useful knowledge or helpful experience.

XXXIV

OF FISH COOKERY

FISH has of late become a more popular article of diet than it used to be, partly owing to the greater variety offered, and also because facilities of transport bring it to market in far better condition. There is still, however, much room for improvement in the matter of cost, and for education in the methods of treatment.

No reader of Pierre Loti's *Pêcheur d'Islande* can see the great cod on the fishmongers' slabs without remembering his moving descriptions of toil and danger in Northern seas, whilst the crabs and lobsters, the red mullet and iridescent mackerel, recall pages of romance from the vivid pen of Victor Hugo. High tea with its fresh herrings, and the worker's supper of bloater or kipper, hold an added interest when we conjure up a vision of harbour quays in the far Shetlands, where brown sails are furled, and Scotch fisher-girls with bare feet, shawled, hooded, and kilted high, work with dexterous swiftness, whilst the sea-gulls cry and flock and hover under the grey skies.

The following recipes for fish cookery may be useful in popularizing what is " halesome farin' " as well as " lives o' men."

This family bowl of economical but excellent *Cod's Head Soup* can be recommended.

Fry in a stewpan large enough to hold a medium-sized cod's head, 2 chopped onions to a golden brown, add 2 dessert-spoonfuls flour, 1 teaspoonful curry powder, all stirred together, and then the cod's head added. Just cover with water, add 3 sliced tomatoes, a bouquet of thyme, parsley, bay leaf, and let them all simmer gently for from 2 to 3 hours. Strain through a sieve, return soup to stewpan, season with salt and pepper, boil up, and before serving add some cooked vermicelli or some croutons of bread.

Fried Fillets à la Orly of whiting, plaice, or lemon soles, for a family dinner-party.

Lay as many fillets of fish as required in a dish and marinade for an hour with a little olive oil, and a few slices of carrot, onion, thyme, and parsley sprinkled over. Make a batter, allowing 6 table-spoonfuls flour, 1 teaspoonful salad oil; mix with a little cold water. Add the whites of 2 eggs whipped stiffly, dip each fillet into the batter, and fry deep in hot lard until golden brown and crackling crisply. Put the remaining batter into a colander, and stir with a wooden spoon into the hot fat and fry a golden colour, looking like large field peas in size, but brown. Drain and dish the fillets on to a hot dish, sprinkle over the fried bits of batter, and some fried parsley or celery tops, and serve very hot, with quarters of lemon, or with a cold anchovy sauce made by whipping not too stiffly 1s. worth of cream, adding very gradually a teaspoonful of anchovy essence, one of the simplest, best, and but rarely seen, fish sauces.

Cold Crab Soufflé, for a summer luncheon-party of eight.

Take a crab weighing about 3½ lb. Remove all fish from the shell and one
claw ; put into a basin, season with salt
and pepper, add a teacupful of mayonnaise sauce and one of liquid aspic jelly.
Mix all well together, and stir in 4 leaves
of dissolved gelatine. Lay at the bottom
of a fluted white china or silver soufflé
dish some lettuce leaves, shredded, and
some slices of tomato ; half fill with the
prepared crab, then cover over with part
of the meat flaked from the other claw,
cover with the rest of the mixture, then
the rest of the claw. Leave this to set.
Before serving it very cold cover the top
of the soufflé with finely-chopped aspic
jelly, and send round sandwiches of
brown or white bread with green filling.

There are so many nice ways of cooking
soles that it is difficult to make choice, but
for a small informal party of six or eight
who appreciate a good fish course this recipe
is offered.

Soles à la Dorchester.

Fold in half required number of fillets
of sole and poach them carefully. Lay
them in a round buttered fireproof or

glass oven dish, and sprinkle freely with some previously cooked and cut up asparagus sprue, or tips (or green peas). Pour over some good béchamel sauce, to which about a tablespoonful of grated parmesan has been added. Put into the oven till slightly browned, and serve in the same dish. The same fillets might be served *à la Dorothéa*, on a round metal dish with a suspicion of tomato sauce about their moist and creamily poached folds, lying round a timbale of savoury yellowish rice, enriched with plenty of butter and seasoning, and a pinch of saffron, a suspicion of the same rather thick tomato sauce, and a certainty of finely-chopped mushrooms, or, if permissible, of truffle peelings.

A holiday luxury for schoolroom tea of *Potted Shrimps* is best made at home.

Take 1s. worth of freshly picked shrimps and wash them in a little warm water; drain, dry, and pound them lightly, leaving a few whole. Work in enough fresh butter to lubricate and bind them, with some pepper and salt, and press them into a wide-topped shallow pot or jar, cover with clarified butter. Or if for *immediate* use, substitute for the covering butter a little thick cream, salted and peppered. Any fragments of salmon or lobster might be worked in with advantage, but shrimps keep fresh a shorter time than these, which is against mixing them, unless for prompt consumption.

Consideration for the reader precludes further suggestions, but having enjoyed these, there is the comfortable reflection that the ocean is as fertile as the land, and that there are " as good fish in the sea as ever came out of it " ; a blessed truth which our coward spirits are tempted to doubt or even to deny.

XXXV

SOME EASTER SWEETS

FOOD for thought is the daily and often distasteful portion of all, but thought for food is the housekeeper's prerogative, and one which she will the more joyfully exercise when prices drop with the approach of summer, when milk, cream, and butter get every day more plentiful, and hens lay their best Easter eggs with commendable diligence. Suggestions for some nice sweet dishes specially suitable to that festive season will not perhaps be inappropriate. First, then, a dish of *Méringues* for Spring's birthday party, and be sure you get the mixture right, not white, chalky, oversweet, but slightly sticky and soft, below a thin crisp outside shell of the complexion of the weakest *café-au-lait* imaginable, and cooked freshly, not dried over-

251

night in the oven as some ordain. This formula for a dish of the usual small type of méringues is generally successful, but a suitable oven temperature is the ruling factor, and here practice and experience, the only trustworthy guides, alone can teach.

Four whites of egg, ¾ lb. white sugar, less one large tablespoonful. Beat the whites first, adding sugar slowly, beating all the time. Work away hard at this till all the sugar is incorporated and the mixture stiff so that the whisk refuses to function. Put the half méringues in heaped tablespoonfuls on to a *wooden* board, and cook in a very slow oven from 30 to 60 minutes. Shape if necessary, fill with whipped cream flavoured vanilla, chocolate, orange, or violet, and join two together.

For the latest fashion in this sweet—the large *Gala Méringue*—

Make 2 flat méringues about the size of a pudding or meat plate, according to requirement, in the usual way with the whites of 5 eggs and 10 oz. sugar. Whisk stiffly ¾ pint cream, incorporate into it some fruit, such as white grapes, skinned, pipped, but not quite divided, and some bananas sliced into shillings, or thinly-cut canned apricots or peaches, or bottled maraschino cherries might be used, or fresh strawberries. Spread the lower méringue to the depth of 1 inch with this sandwich mixture of cream and fruit, and cover it lightly with the other méringue, serving on a napkin in a large round silver or decorative china dish.

Here is a recipe for *Caramel of Eggs*, a sweet suitable for a refined little luncheon or dinner of six, and calculated to give an impression of largesse unwarranted by fact. Indeed, bets have been won on the number of eggs required, and the cost of the pudding thereby reduced !

Whip 3 whites of eggs very stiff, incorporating 3 oz. castor sugar as for méringue. Line a small charlotte mould throughout with a thin caramel of burnt sugar and water, and let this just set ; pour in the egg froth and steam very gently in a large stewpan for 1 hour ; let it cool in the stewpan for 1 hour. Make a custard with the 3 yolks, adding ½ pint cream, or cream and milk mixed, flavour nicely with crushed vanilla pod or essence, and sweeten and pour round

253

the now firm white island flecked with caramel turned out into a silver dish, and serve very cold. Any nice compote of fruit could advantageously, though not necessarily, accompany this sweet ; or some of these home-made

Macaroon Biscuits.

A ¼ lb. ground almonds, ½ lb. icing sugar, 2 whites of eggs whipped and 2 unwhipped ; bake about 20 minutes and put half an almond on the top whilst still soft. Or for a harder variety of macaroon, try ¼ lb. ground almonds, ½ lb. castor sugar, ½ oz. rice flour, essence of vanilla to flavour, 3 small whites, all well beaten for 10 minutes, placed on round rice papers in spoonfuls, and baked 20 minutes.

This *Bombe Néro* was one of the successes of the artist chef of the Cannes Casino during a recent conference :—

Make a round fresh madeira or sponge mixture cake, scoop out the inside, and fill in with some good vanilla ice cream. Cover with méringue, put the dish that it is to be served in in a deep tin, well packed with broken ice, in a quick oven till the méringue is lightly browned—2 minutes or less should suffice—withdraw and place on a larger dish, pouring round a few tablespoonfuls of old rum or brandy warmed, and set this alight at the dining-room door.

Our American friends have a variety of this, known as *Baked Alaska,* the cake omitted, the central mound of fruit-flavoured ice cream coloured pink, the méringue mixture thrown over it more copiously, and a little thin maple syrup sauce, fruit flavoured and also coloured pink to accompany in a bowl.

The following *Pears en Surprise* we owe to the abundant modern importations of sweet nicely-shaped Cape dessert pears :—

Peel and stew the required number, not too soft (leaving on the stalk), in a syrup flavoured with lemon peel and cloves. When cold, cut off the top 1 inch below stalk, scoop out centre of lower part, fill in with vanilla-flavoured whipped or iced cream, replace the top, adding a ruffle of stiffly-whipped-vanilla cream, and stand the fat end of each pear on a toasted round of cake soaked with a little sherry. Serve in a glass dish with the surrounding syrup.

To close on a note of moderation, enabling the cook to make a nice Sunday sweet before she goes out, here is a good *Cold Lemon Soufflé*.

> Take the yolks of 3 eggs, the juice of 3 lemons, and grated rind of 2, with ½ lb. loaf sugar, about 1 tablespoonful of gelatine dissolved in milk. Stir all over the fire till it thickens. Whip ½ pint cream and beat up the whites of the 3 eggs stiffly and stir these gently into the custard mixture. Pour all into a soufflé dish, and sprinkle with chopped pistachio or crushed ratafia, and serve very cold.

This series of recipes and suggestions is now, with apologies for any imperfections, brought to a close, remembering that it is better to turn off the tap whilst yet there is water in the cistern. Did not the Princess Grania, when asked by her lover Diarmid which was the best of jewels, reply, " The knife "—a saying to be noted by men, women, and writers. Echoing then the words of a great teacher but lately gone from us, this writer would say in farewell, " Some authors expect fame, others desire gold. I shall be content with forgiveness."

INDEX OF RECIPES

(2,307)

R

INDEX OF RECIPES

INDEX OF RECIPES

INDEX OF RECIPES

INDEX OF RECIPES

INDEX OF RECIPES

INDEX OF RECIPES

THE END.